contents

iv **Preface**
by Michael DeMarco, M.A.

v **Author Bio Notes**

CHAPTERS

1 Nihonto: A Legal Perspective on Japanese Swords and Their Intrinsic Value
by Andrew Tharp, B.S.

16 Oshigata: Appreciating Japanese Sword Tracings for Their Reference and Beauty
by Anthony DiCristofano

21 Bladed Weaponry with Illustrations from the Japanese Antique Sword Museum
by Harunaka Hoshino

41 Amateur Saya Craft: Scabbards in the Making
by Richard W. Babin

61 Sword-Cutting Practice of Feudal Japan: Anatomical Considerations of Tameshigiri
by Peter J. Ward, Ph.D.

81 The Ainu and Their Swords in Japan: A Concise Overview
by Curt Peritz

96 1,000 Swordmaking Cuts: August Events at the Kingfisher Woodworks
by James Goedkoop, B.A.

105 **Index**

preface

The famed samurai sword (*nihonto*) represents the pinnacle of bladed weaponry in the Japanese warrior's arsenal. Gifted smiths ingeniously designed the weapon with supremely subtle details to make these swords most efficient killing tools. Whenever the topic of samurai culture is mentioned, the usual image that comes to mind is of a flourishing scene of mortal combat, glimmering swords, and sprays of crimson blood. This book has a different focus: it addresses the sword's intrinsic historic, monetary, military, and artistic values.

Seven chapters provide much information for readers to gain insight and appreciation of the samurai sword. The writings for this particular anthology were selected from materials published in the *Journal of Asian Martial Arts* and are organized thematically so readers will gradually—chapter by chapter—gain a panoramic view of the sword with an artist's eye.

Tharp's work provides a fine introductory chapter as he details aspects of the nihonto that make it unique in the world as a valued *objet d'art*, protected by law codes specifically written to preserve these cultural relics even when made by contemporary master smiths.

The following chapter by DiCristofano is on *oshigata*, or sword sketchings, which allow the human eye to view details of the sword blade often unnoticed because of the subtlety inherent in the work. The sketches highlight the tempering patterns that result from the forging process and other characteristics, such as polishing and etching. When illustrated by a competent artist, the resulting sketches view like X-rays of blades, worthy of display in their own right.

Hoshino's chapter presents a overview of various blade types, including nihonto, spears, halberds, knives, guards, and dressings. Basic categories of bladed weaponry are discussed as well as the stages of swordsmithing. His focus on blades leads to the next chapter by Richard Babin on how to make a scabbard—a home for the blade! Since scabbards are often damaged while protecting blades, this proves to be a particularly useful chapter, as many practitioners can make their own scabbard as a replacement or just to enjoy the craftwork.

The design and making of nihonto stem from the most practical use in warfare. How well do they actually work? "Test cutting" (*tameshigiri*) provides proof. It was common to use the bodies of executed criminals to test the cutting abilities of swords and the swordsmen themselves. Peter Ward utilized an ancient diagram of sixteen main targets for body cuts and modern technology to actually view the inner structures of the blade's path along these targets. This gives a deep

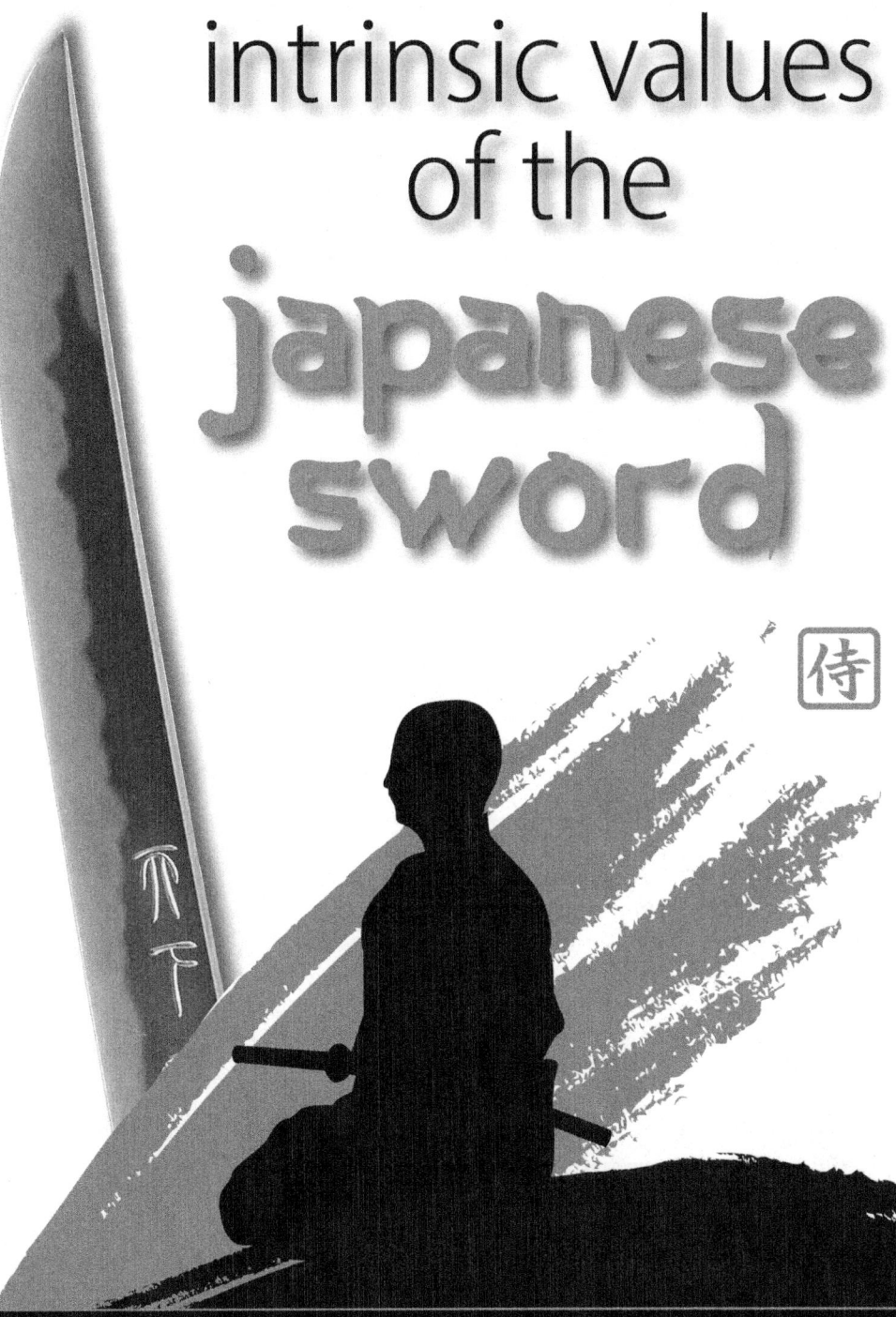

intrinsic values of the japanese sword

An Anthology of Articles from the *Journal of Asian Martial Arts*
Edited by Michael A. DeMarco, M.A.

Disclaimer
Please note that the authors and publisher of this book are not responsible in any manner whatsoever for any injury that may result from practicing the techniques and/or following the instructions given within. Since the physical activities described herein may be too strenuous in nature for some readers to engage in safely, it is essential that a physician be consulted prior to training.

All Rights Reserved
No part of this publication, including illustrations, may be reproduced or utilized in any form or by any means, electronic or mechanical, including photocopying, recording, or by any information storage and retrieval system (beyond that copying permitted by sections 107 and 108 of the US Copyright Law and except by reviewers for the public press), without written permission from Via Media Publishing Company.

Warning: Any unauthorized act in relation to a copyright work may result in both a civil claim for damages and criminal prosecution.

Copyright © 2015 by
Via Media Publishing Company
941 Calle Mejia #822
Santa Fe, NM 87501 USA
E-mail: md@goviamedia.com

All articles in this anthology were originally published in the *Journal of Asian Martial Arts*. Listed according to the table of contents for this anthology:

Tharp, A. (2012)	Volume 21, Number 1	pages 56–71
DiChristofano, A. (2011)	Volume 20, Number 3	pages 86–91
Hoshino, H. (1993)	Volume 2, Number 1	pages 92–108
Babin, R. (2000)	Volume 9, Number 4	pages 36–51
Ward, P. (2003)	Volume 22, Number 1	pages 1–18
Peritz, C. (1994)	Volume 3, Number 1	pages 26–39
Goedkoop, J. (2003)	Volume 12, Number 2	pages 40–47

Book and cover design by Via Media Publishing Company

Edited by Michael A. DeMarco, M.A.

Cover illustrations

Photograph of blade courtesy of Anthony DiChristofano • www.namahagesword.com
Illustration courtesy of Dreamstime.com

ISBN: 978-1893765-16-0

www.viamediapublishing.com

understanding of just what the sword wielded by skilled hands confronts: bone, muscle, tendon, and organs in differing degrees of resistance to cutting.

A special chapter presents the Ainu, an indigenous group in Japan with a separate heritage from the Japanese. They were noted for their own flavor of design, which influenced their use of weapons as well. Famed for woodcarving, they did not possess the technology to produce metal. As a result they incorporated blades made by Japanese smiths according to their own taste. Author Curt Peritz also includes details of the centuries of bitter skirmishes between the Ainu and expanding Japanese forces.

The above chapter overview focuses on the metal blades that made nihonto treasured by scholars, practitioners, and collectors. The final chapter, by James Goedkoop, deals with another medium, as the master craftsman creates wooden replicas of Japanese swords. Of course there are differences between sword smithing and woodcarving, but there are similarities too. Read this chapter and see how an uncarved piece of wood becomes an exquisite sword, perfectly shaped and exhibiting its fine grain sealed with teak oil.

This anthology should be an informative, enjoyable read. As you read other books and articles about Japanese swords, or practice kendo or iaido, or see highly polished blades in a museum, the chapters here will enhance your knowledge and appreciation of nihonto and their intrinsic value.

Michael A. DeMarco
Santa Fe, NM
October 2015

author bio notes

- **Richard W. Babin, B.S., M.D.,** is a practicing surgeon who served two years' active duty in the USAF as chief of head and neck surgery at Maxwell Field during the Vietnam conflict. His interest in the martial arts began with several years of judo in the 1960s in San Francisco. Upon entering private practice he began studying Yang-style taiji. He has practiced Muso Shinden Ryu iaido for many years and has been awarded the rank of third dan by the All US Kendo Federation.
- **Anthony DiCristofano** studied Japanese language and kendo before heading off to Japan in 1993. He returned to Japan in 2005 in order to observe and learn traditional Japanese foundation forging and to study and understand the process of making traditional Japanese steel (tamahagane). Among his noted teachers are Leon Kapp, and Master Smith Yoshindo Yoshihara (designated Important Intangible Cultural Asset by the Japanese government). Since 2000 he's been a professional smith.
- **James Goedkoop, B.A.,** runs Kingfisher WoodWorks LLC in Vermont, manufacturing wooden weapons specific to the Japanese sword-related martial arts. He produced the bokken used on the set of Edward Zwick's movie The Last Samurai. The chapter in this e-book documents an evolution into the redevelopment of archaic techniques in weapons production. Goedkoop's mastery of woodworking is married to the subtle sensitivities of Japanese aesthetics and budo.
- **Harunaka Hoshino** trained in karate, kenjutsu, and ninjutsu in Tokyo, Japan. His martial arts background is balanced with studies in Japanese culture, history, and language. Mr. Hoshino serves as the president of the Japanese Sword Society and Japanese Sword Restoration Center.
- **Curt Peritz** spent decades researching the history and culture of the Ainu, an indigenous people of Japan. Because of the Ainus' particular flair for woodcarving and adapting Japanese sword blades to fit their own style of sword dressing, he conducted research in Japan as well as a number of museums, such as the Peabody Museum in Salem, Massachusetts. Mr. Peritz's chapter embodies the results of his years of research.
- **Andrew Tharp, J.D.,** earned juris doctorate degree from the Indiana University Maurer School of Law in 2012. In addition, he holds a B.S. in business and a certificate in martial arts from Indiana University. He has practiced a variety of weapon based arts including: iaido, taijiquan, Filipino stick arts, and German longsword. He served as the senior fencing instructor for Indiana University from 2007 until 2012.
- **Peter J. Ward, M.S., Ph.D.,** has studied a variety of Japanese martial arts, including jujutsu, kenjutsu, jojutsu, and atemijutsu. He received his degree in human anatomy from Perdue University. Dr. Ward taught Human Gross Anatomy for Medial Students at Indiana University School of Medicine and is now an associate professor of anatomy at the West Virginia School of Osteopathic Medicine.

Nihonto: A Legal Perspective on Japanese Swords and Their Intrinsic Value

by Andrew Tharp, B.S.

Above scene is from the graphic novel series,
Tales of the Hermit, by O. Ratti and A. Westbrook.
© Futuro Designs and Publications.

The sword is a powerful symbol. For as long as civilization can remember, it has represented war, nobility, power, and justice. Yet all cultures have modified, enhanced, or fixed the sword to mold to their way of life. The symbol of the sword is ever prevalent, but always uniquely represented. Japan has always had a particular reverence for the sword. The *nihonto*, commonly called the samurai sword, has always been a source of pride for the Japanese people. This is not to say the European sword is any less important or potent, but that Western culture did not embrace the sword with the same fervor as the Japanese.

Note: The term *nihonto* can include several different kinds of swords from Japan—while most people associate it with the longsword (*katana*), it can also be applied to the short sword (*wakizashi*), or the knife-sized sword (*tanto*).

Nihonto hold a special position in Japanese history. They are not just weapons of war; they are artwork, pieces of jewelry, symbols of status, and representations of the "soul of the samurai" (Yumoto, 1997). There are traditional martial arts, theater, artwork, and etiquette centered entirely on the sword (Yumoto, 1997: 12). Japanese smiths sign each sword they make, and the swords are often given names by their owners (Ratti & Westbrook, 1991). Some swords used in World War II had been passed down from warrior generation to warrior generation for over six hundred years (Yumoto, 1997: 12). Those smiths who make the best swords each year have work that is forever enshrined as a national treasure. In fact, some swordsmiths have even attained the rank of "living national treasure" for their contributions to the arts (Agency, website). There is even a government organization that has the sole responsibility of the registration and preservation of the Japanese sword (Nihon Bujutsu, website). As a result of such reverence, to this day Japan has the most well-preserved swords in the world, both in quality and quantity.

Why is that the case? An intense analysis of both the culture of the Japanese sword as well as the legal systems that surround it will attempt to answer that question. First we will examine the culture that surrounds the sword and its history, and then we will look at three specific legal elements. The first is about the registration of swords, the second concerns the import and export of swords, and the third is centered on the manufacture of swords.

Japanese Sword History and Culture

The history of the Japanese sword could, and has, filled many books, but this section will attempt to distill the most important information. For the purposes of this essay, the Japanese sword will refer only to *nihonto* (or Japanese-made swords, as opposed to Japanese styled swords, not made in Japan). Like many other aspects of Japanese culture, nihonto evolution demonstrates a decided cycle of massive change, followed by long periods of stagnancy. This can likely be traced back to both the lack of trade and a culture of isolation, which created a relatively unchanged and singular form of sword.

The most common form of the Japanese sword is a single-bladed sword of about thirty inches, designed for use with one or two hands (Yumoto, 1997: 24). Like the Western sword, the Japanese sword has undergone several reincarnations. As with many other aspects of Japanese culture, the sword was imported from China in its infancy (Yumoto, 1997: 23). The earliest Japanese swords were very similar to Chinese swords from the same period (generally anytime before CE 650). It was not until the Heian period (794 to 1191) that Japanese swords began to take on what is now their distinct form (Yumoto, 1997: 24). During this period the primary form of warfare was mounted (Yumoto, 1997: 24). The curvature of the sword was more suited to slashing from horseback than were the previous straight swords, used primarily for stabbing. The swords of this period are generally referred to as *tachi*, and were worn with the blade facing downward, much like the early modern cavalry saber (Ratti & Westbrook, 1991: 256).

Later the sword evolved into what is now typically called the *katana* (Ratti & Westbrook, 1991: 256). The sword kept its characteristic curvature, but the need for mounted combat fell dramatically. At this point, the sword took on an entirely different place. It was shortened and worn blade up in the belt, rather than blade down. It was carried as a self-defense weapon by the samurai and was superseded as the primary weapon of war. The *naginata* (halberd) and *yumi* (bow and arrow) took its place (Yumoto, 1997: 24). The European sword also saw a similar evolution, but the katana continued to retain its curvature, whereas most self-defense swords in Europe relied on the point of the weapon (Oakeshott, 2007). Why nihonto retained their curved, cutting-focused structure is up for debate, but it probably has to do with both the manufacture of the weapons as well as the culture surrounding them.

When outlining the manufacture of a Japanese sword, it is important to note that there are many artisans who devote their entire lives in training to make each part of the sword. In this article we will focus on the forging of the blade, but there are also individuals who polish and sharpen swords, make the handle and guard (known as the "furniture"), and make the scabbard. A completed sword includes work by all of these artisans. It is also important to note at this point the seriousness with which a smith undertakes his work. Like most Japanese craftsmen, the swordsmith has a patron deity. Every forge has a deity shelf, where prayers are offered before, during, and after the creation of the sword. Swordsmiths believe they have divine assistance when creating their works (Yumoto, 1997: 99).

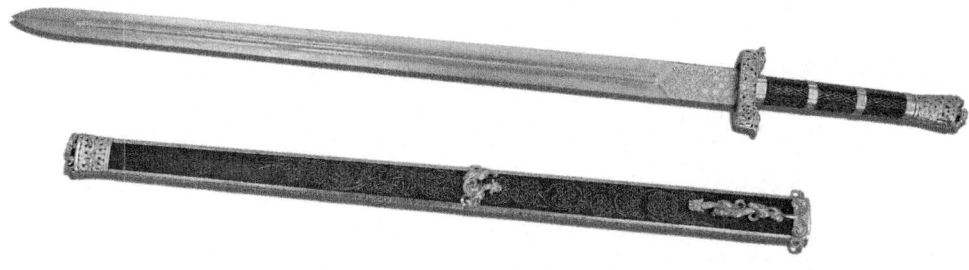

This sword is a recreation of what would have been common in the Han period of China (206 BCE–200 CE) It is would have been very similar to early period Japanese swords.

A wooden display stand for a tanto and it fittings.

There are generally considered to be four steps in forging a blade (Ratti & Westbrook, 1991: 259). The first is rough forging. This is when the traditional iron (*tamahagane*) is treated to create steel. The iron is heated and then folded, and the process is repeated twelve to fifteen times. This creates between 4,000 and 32,000 layers. This is also the process that creates the *hada*, or grain, within the blade. The heating and fold take the carbon that lies dormant in the charcoal and infuse it with the iron, creating steel. After the rough forging, the steel is shaped into the final form desired by the smith. The steel pieces are heated and fused together to make a billet of sword-shaped steel. Next is the clay covering and heating process. The blade is covered in a thin layer of clay, the composition of which is generally proprietary to the smith. The clay layer is generally thinner toward the blade (*ha*) and heavier toward the back (*mune*). Next, the clay-covered sword is heated in a kiln. The final step is the quenching of the blade. The heated blade is submerged, typically in saltwater, although, like the clay, many smiths use different mixtures. The clay makes the blade cool unevenly, creating both the curvature of the blade and the dividing line between the hard and soft sections of the blade (*hamon*). At this point, the completed blade is sent to the polisher for finishing (Yumoto, 1997: 98–109).

The forging of the sword is essential to its form, but so is the culture that surrounds it. The traditional martial arts of the Japanese sword are *kendo* and *iaido* (before the U.S. occupation in World War II, they were called *kenjutsu* and *iaijutsu*) (Ratti & Westbrook, 1991: 24). Like most traditional elements of

Japanese culture, these arts are ritualistic and steeped in mysticism, but highly effective. Iaido is a key element to the form of the Japanese sword. The slightly curved blade with a long handle is the only acceptable shape that allows for the fluid motions of drawing and sheathing the blade that are the foundation of iaido (Suino, 2004). This fact shows one of the many cultural reasons the Japanese sword has remained in a similar state for over six hundred years. While it is probably impossible to argue the superiority of the Japanese systems of swordsmanship, it is evident that martial arts and other cultural norms have influenced the sword. Although it has certainly gone through some changes, what is most significant about the Japanese sword are the ways in which it has remained the same.

Tamahagane (a) must be purchased from the NBTHK. After heating in a furnace (b), two pieces of harder steel are being folded with a softer piece in the middle (c). This gives the final sword flexibility as well as hardness. It also allows the sword to both hold a razor sharp edge, but not snap when put under pressure.

The modern view of the weapon is significantly different from the historical perspective, but it is still essential to understanding why the nihonto has survived this long and is still being manufactured and preserved with traditional methods. In the West the sword died long ago. While weapons were still commonly issued in the American Civil War, most mortal wounds did not come from swords (Sayers, website). From the time of the American Civil War to World War I the sword almost entirely disappeared from the battlefield. This is mostly attributable to the invention of the repeating pistol as a sidearm (Britannica, website). The reduction in cavalry led to a near extinction of the sword on the battlefield. Today many militaries use swords as a uniform piece for formal occasions, but they have not been routinely used on the battlefield in more than a century (Britannica, website).

This is not true in Japan, where even up until the end of World War II the Japanese military was still carrying and using swords.

Again, this derives from an intense need for constancy and strong traditionalism. The warrior caste (*bushi*) of Japan carried swords for most of its history. The sword was carried as a mark of nobility and station (Yumoto, 1997: 12). There were, again, strong traditions related to the wearing, removing, and carrying of the sword. Wearing the sword was an art in itself, with as much depth and importance as the art of actually using the blade. Whether or not the sword was actually an effective weapon on the modern battlefield was irrelevant. Members of the new warrior caste (military officers) not only desired but were expected to wear the weapons of their forefathers. In some cases, they were even wearing the physical weapons of their forefathers, as many swords had been passed down for generations and were simply refitted to modern military standards (Yumoto, 1997: 13).

Today the sword lives on in the popular culture of Japan. Many movies, anime, and books prominently feature the nihonto, and museums feature huge displays of antique blades (NBTHK, website). This is not so different from the West, where our popular culture also often centers on the sword, but there is a major difference. Collectors of Western swords are generally considered collectors of militaria or antiquity. Collectors of nihonto are considered art collectors. This may not seem like a major difference, but in effect, it creates a whole new dynamic to the market and preservation of the weapons. In general, nihonto are not only collected for their historical value, but also for their intrinsic beauty (Yumoto, 1997: 15). Today some modern smiths can still charge upwards of $10,000 for a modern-made blade with no military value. Nihonto are traded and auctioned as pieces of fine art and given the same valuations. Unlike Western swords, they are not traded based on what pattern or military used them, or what engagements they might have been involved in, but rather on what swordsmith (artist) made them, as well as the quality of the hada and hamon. Today a quality nihonto is incredibly expensive and takes an expert to determine its value (Yumoto, 1997: 95).

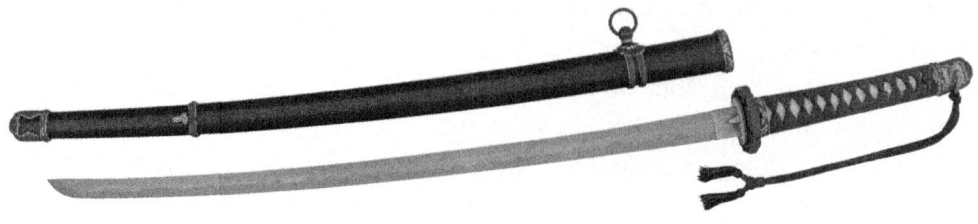

This picture shows a recreation of a *gunto*, which is the name commonly given to the swords carried by Japanese soldiers in World War II.

Although the culture of the nihonto is somewhat different from that of the Western European sword, it cannot account for all of the differences in the preservation and reverence of the sword. Rather, there are several legal aspects as well. In general, one of the most important elements is the governmental protection of nihonto. The primary protection comes from the Agency for Cultural Affairs.

The Agency for Cultural Affairs

The Agency for Cultural Affairs (ACA) was formed following WWII as a way to preserve traditional Japanese culture in the wake of the massive destruction of the war (Agency, website: 5). One of the primary responsibilities of the ACA was creating the system of categorizing and managing cultural properties. That responsibility manifested itself through the list of "Cultural Properties of Japan." The list contains assets of Japanese history and culture deemed to be of the utmost importance and worthy of protection. It is divided into two categories: tangible and intangible cultural properties (Agency, website: 2).

Tangible cultural properties are temples, shrines, residences, castles, crafts, and archeological artifacts. These items are further subdivided based on their relative importance. They are either categorized as "highly important" or "national treasures" (Agency, website: 4). Currently there are 110 swords and twelve sets of sword mountings on the list of registered national treasures (Wikipedia, National Treasures). In addition to tangible cultural assets, sword making is among the original crafts listed a "highly important" intangible cultural asset. People, as well as crafts, can be deemed intangible cultural assets. Colloquially called "living national treasures," these individuals have mastered the crafts considered fundamental to Japanese culture (Agency, website: 10). Any individual named a living national treasure receives an annual government grant to continue his or her craft. There are currently three individuals who fall under the category of sword making on the list, and there have been a total of ten individuals named living national treasures for their work with swords (Wikipedia, National Treasures).

The closest organization that could be compared with the ACA in the United States would be the National Park Service. Although both are tasked with preserving important culture and icons throughout the country, there are significant differences. The first and most important is likely the lack of a list of tangible cultural properties in the United States. There are several lists, such as the National Register of Historic Places, but none of them includes privately owned objects (16 U.S.C. 470). In addition, the protections that the Japanese place upon items listed as national treasures are far more restrictive than those in the United States (Agency, website: 5).

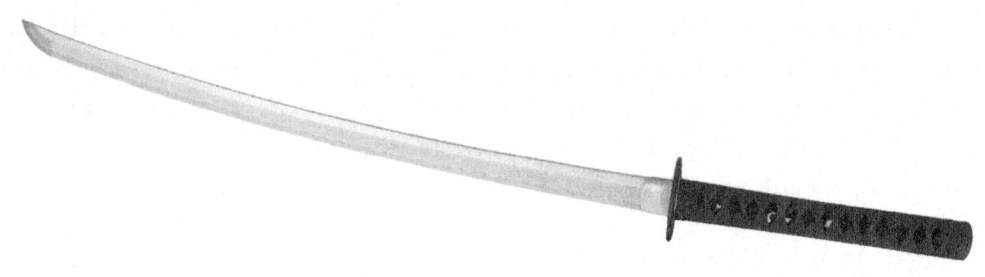

This *Tori katana* is made by CAS Hanwei in a similar fashion as a traditional nihonto, but is available for a fraction of the price. The cost difference is in part due to the artificial demand created by the Japanese culture and government. The value of a nihonto is not the extrinsic value of a well-made sword, but rather the intrinsic value of their artistry, history, and culture.

The general administration of the nihonto aspects of the list of cultural properties is left up to a separate organization, the Nihon Bijutsu Token Hozon Kyokai (NBTHK). The NBTHK is not a government organization, but is an authorized foundation, and it determines whether items are considered "highly important" or "national treasures" under the definitions set forth by the ACA (Nihon Bujutsu, website).

The Nihon Bijutsu Token Hozon Kyokai
Immediately following World War II, the United States occupied Japan. During this occupation, there was a universal ban on weapons, and this included nihonto. The servicemen of the United States occupation force destroyed or removed over half a million Japanese swords during this time. As a response to this assault on their traditions, the Japanese formed the Nihon Bijutsu Token Hozon Kyokai (NBTHK).

The NBTHK is the Society for the Preservation of Japanese Art Swords. As described, the Japanese truly feel that the swords are a traditional part of Japanese culture and are works of art, but it was difficult for the United States occupation force to understand the significance. In response, the NBTHK was founded to create an ambassador to the occupation force and attempt to stop the destruction of traditional Japanese weapons (NBTHK European, website).

This was not a strategy unique to the weapons themselves, but was also utilized in the practice of traditional sword arts, as well as other traditional martial arts. The suffix generally affixed to martial arts was *–jutsu*, which means "technique." During the occupation, the native practitioners began to refer to their arts with the suffix *–do*, which means "way." Thus, *kenjutsu* (the technique of the sword) became *kendo* (the way of the sword), and *jujutsu* (the gentle technique) became *judo* (the gentle way). By changing the names of the traditional arts of their culture, the Japanese managed to prevent the occupational forces from destroying some of most important aspects of their history (Ratti & Westbrook, 1991: 24).

Today, the NBTHK has eight primary activities and services (NBTHK European, website):

1) **The Conservation Project of Japanese Art Swords:** The NBTHK will issue certificates and registrations to swords, as well as give them a class. The classes are hozon token (worthy of preservation or authentic), tokubetsu hozon token (high quality and worthy of preservation), juyo token (historically important and authentic), or tokubetsu juyo hozon (historically important as well as high quality).

2) **Shinshakuto Exhibition:** Shinshakuto are newly made swords, and this exhibition is presented each year to show the best swordsmiths' work. Each year swords are awarded first, second, and third place, as well as nyusen, which means they were accepted to the competition. All the swords accepted to the competition are shown in the NBTHK museum. Swords are judged solely on their artistic value.

3) **Sword Polishing and Furniture Competition:** Similar to the forging competition, swords polishers and mounters are judged on the quality of their work.

4) **Tamahagane Smelter:** The NBTHK operates the smelter from which all swordsmiths receive their raw iron.

5) **Seminars:** Seminars in all of the traditional crafts surrounding sword making are given each year.

6) **Education:** The NBTHK offers classes for individuals interested in learning more about the artistic value of swords and how to value them. They also operate the Nihonto Museum in Tokyo.

7) **Magazine:** The NBTHK publishes a monthly magazine dedicated to the nihonto.

8) **Subsidies:** The NBTHK awards subsidies to those who practice the traditional crafting of Japanese swords to continue the tradition of excellence.

The most important responsibilities of the NBTHK are the shinshakuto competition and the conservation project. The shinshakuto competition gives basis for the awards given through the ACA, and the conservation project allows for swords to be given the required papers (*origami*) that legally make them into artwork.

Registering Nihonto

Although guns and swords are substantially different, especially in a Japanese context, they are both weapons and are generally regarded under the same or similar statutes. The primary statute for the possession of swords falls under the Act for Controlling the Possession of Firearms or Swords and Other Such Weapons (Act for Controlling, website). In most circumstances, it is illegal to possess either swords or guns in Japan, but there are various exceptions (Act for Controlling, website).

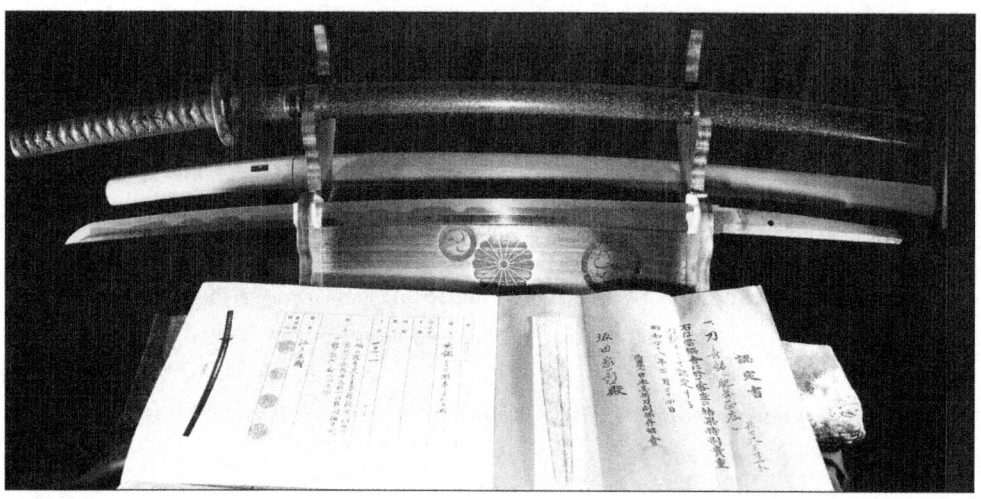

This is a photograph of an authentic nihonto from the early 17th century. This blade is a "first generation" sword (*shodai*) from the Hizen smithing tradition. Below the blade you can see the traditional origami that must be included for a sword to be owned, transported, or imported to Japan.

The primary exceptions allow for weapons to be possessed if they are used for "applications such as hunting, eradication of noxious birds and animals, slaughter of animals, fishing or construction, cases where possession is unavoidable due to Japanese customs and practice, cases where possession is unavoidable for plays or other artistic performances, and cases where such items are used for display in museums" (Act for Controlling, website, 4[2]i). In addition, weapons may be possessed if they have artistic or antique value (Act for Controlling, website, 4[2]i). The second exception is where most Japanese citizens find their right to have nihonto.

In order for a Japanese citizen to own a sword that is exempted for the reason of artistic or antique value, he or she must have it registered with the local prefecture board of education (Act for Controlling, website, [2]). The ACA is a special body of the Japanese Ministry of Education (Agency, website, 1). Since the ACA utilizes the NBTHK to determine which swords are of artistic value, a petitioner must prove to the prefecture board of education that the sword he or she possesses is registered with the NBTHK, generally with origami presented to the owner after appraisal.

In the end, through the creation of the NBTHK and laws of registration, a very effective form of weapon registration was created that did not demean the historical importance of the nihonto. The Japanese have always felt that the nihonto is an important part of their culture, but the U.S. occupational forces were very strict about the kinds of weapons that could be owned by individuals. By putting these protections in place the NBTHK created an effective compromise for both parties. In fact, in traditional Japanese fashion, it made the owners of the swords feel as though registration were both an honor and a duty, because their nihonto were of important historical significance.

The closest direct comparison in the United States would be the National Firearms Act (NFA) (26 U.S.C. ch. 53). The NFA also designates that certain kinds of weapons must be registered with the federal government, but there are substantial differences between the two acts. In the United States, most firearms laws are determined by the states (26 U.S.C. ch. 53). Sword laws are almost non-existent. The NFA only requires registration of a few kinds of weapons, mostly those that have caused problems with law enforcement in the past (26 U.S.C. ch. 53). While the real reason for the two acts may be the same, the sword section of the Japanese act seems to be written more as a way of preserving culture rather than a way of protecting the public.

The act is one of the strongest ways the Japanese have preserved their martial heritage. While it may seem as though requiring the registration and limiting the ability to own a sword would make them scarcer, it has had the opposite effect. Because the Japanese go to such effort to obtain and own these weapons, they have greater incentive to preserve them. In addition, the act provides for a centralized listing of all of the swords, allowing for greater government control and better records of those swords that do still exist.

Importing Nihonto

There are no specific laws about the importing of nihonto, but certain statutes work together to make it impossible to import a non-Japanese blade. The first statute of note is within the act. Section 25 states that a person may not enter Japan with a sword. If a person does, the sword will be confiscated until it is proven to be legal within the country (personal interview with Kazuyo Fujimura, Nov. 16, 2011).

In order for a sword to be legal within the country, as mentioned previously, it must be licensed with the prefecture board of education and have origami issued by the NBTHK (Act at 2). Under this definition, swords are only those made of steel (Act at 4[2]i). In Japan there are many "swords" sold in tourist locations or to practitioners of iaido. These swords, called *mogito*, are generally made of zinc aluminum alloy, and there is no restriction for entering or exiting the country with them (Schiller, website).

The final piece comes from the act itself, which states that "[t]he registration of swords is available for swords which are valuable as works of art, however only Japanese swords have been examined" (Act at 4[2]i). In this case, only a sword that has been registered may be brought into the country. These statutes continue to emphasize the perceived importance and superiority of the nihonto.

Because only nihonto may be kept in Japan, and because the Japanese have such a rich culture of swordsmanship, nihonto remain intact for generations. The only swords available to swordsmen and collectors in Japan are nihonto. Not only that, but the intense regulation of the manufacture of these swords makes them very rare, meaning that antique nihonto are incredibly valuable.

Manufacturing Nihonto

All swords in Japan must be registered, and the registration may only be granted to art swords of Japanese manufacture (Act at 4[2]i). Therefore, all newly made swords, *shinshakuto*, must meet the stringent guidelines of traditional Japanese sword manufacturing, which are enforced by the NBTHK (NBTHK European, website). This creates an effective monopoly on all swordsmithing within Japan.

While the guidelines were originally put in place to encourage tradition, they have created an artificial demand for nihonto that is continuously monitored by the NBTHK. The smiths must follow manufacturing guidelines, the most limiting of which is the use of officially licensed *tamahagane* (NBTHK European, website). The smiths may apply for this tamahagane from the NBTHK, which makes the iron in its smelter. It is the only raw material allowed for manufacture of a true shinshakuto (NBTHK European, website). If a sword is not made out of tamahagane, it will be destroyed immediately (Yoshindo, 1987).

This effectively limits the number of smiths capable of operating within Japan. In addition, the NBTHK limits the number of swords that may be produced. Japanese smiths may only make two swords per month, limiting them to twenty-four per year (Yoshindo, 1987). This is rumored to have been made a rule because the greatest swordsmith of all time, Masamune, took two weeks to make a quality sword. Whether that is true is still up for debate (Yoshindo, 1987: 30).

This artificial monopoly creates great demand for nihonto. Currently, in the United States, if a person wishes to purchase a Japanese styled sword, made by a smith (often trained in Japan), the asking price is between $2,000 and $5,000. If a person wishes to get a Japanese styled sword made in Japan, the asking price is generally at least $10,000 (and if it is made by a renowned smith or is an especially beautiful piece, prices can tip the scales to over $100,000). In addition, the wait time for a shinshakuto is generally between six months and two years, depending on the smith. Swords made in the United States are generally of the same quality, but lack the pedigree and origami of a true nihonto.

Whether or not the NBTHK made these rules as a means to achieve their goals of preservation is unknown, but they have achieved them. With these rules, the value of antique nihonto has skyrocketed, since people have such limited access to newly made pieces. With such high value, the Japanese have worked hard to preserve the swords that they already own, and thus, the NBTHK's goals have been realized.

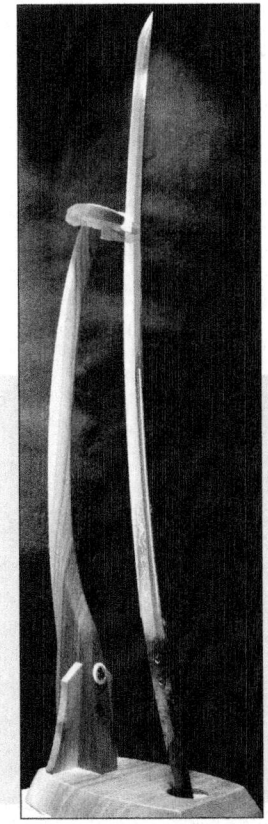

This beautiful nihonto blade shows some of the defining characteristics sought after by collectors, including a *horimono* or blade carving. This particular sword is of the Mihara School and was likely forged between 1350 and 1500.

Conclusion

The Japanese have functionally created a monopoly around one of their greatest cultural assets. The word monopoly is a loaded term, but in this situation, it is not morally objectionable for this monopoly to exist. Although the Japanese have limited importation, manufacture, sale, and possession of this cultural commodity, it has worked to their advantage. Today there are more Japanese swords in excellent condition than any other kind of sword. They are collected, traded, and sought after. This intrinsic value, created by both culture and law, has led to a forced preservation. The governmental concern for this archaic art form has only strengthened the market. By creating this artificial demand, it has led to the conservation of one of Japan's greatest historical assets.

Acknowledgment

A special thanks to Ms. Kazuyo Fujimura, who helped with Japanese translations and statutory interpretations. Photographs of modern replica swords and the forging process were supplied by CAS Hanwei. The photographs of genuine nihonto are courtesy of Mr. James Rosch and are pieces from his personal collection. All photos are property of CAS Hanwei or Mr. James Rosch.

References

Act for Controlling the Possession of Firearms or Swords and Other Such Weapons. Translation available at: http://www8.cao.go.jp/kisei-kaikaku/oto/otodb/english/houseido/hou/ lh_05050.html

Agency for Cultural Affairs, Cultural Properties for Future Generations: Outline of the Cultural Administration of Japan (pamphlet), available at http://www.bunka.go.jp/bunkazai/pamphlet/pdf/pamphlet_en_03_ver03.pdf

Encyclopedia Britannica, Definition: Sword available at: http://www.britannica.com/EBchecked/topic/577385/swordNihon Bujutsu Hozon Token Kyokai Homepage, available at http://www.touken. or.jp/english/index.html

NBTHK American Homepage available at: http://www.nbthk-ab.org/Japan.htm

NBTHK European Branch Homepage available at: http://www.nbthk.net/NBTHKe/NBTHK.html

Nihon Bujutsu Hozon Token Kyokai Homepage, available at http://www.touken.or.jp/english/index.html

Oakeshott, E. (2007). *Records of the medieval sword*. Rochester, NY: Boydell Press.

Ratti, O. & Westbrook, A. (1991). *Secrets of the samurai: The martial arts of feudal*

Japan. Edison, NJ: Castle Books.

Sayers, A. Introduction to Civil War cavalry. Available at: http://ehistory.osu.edu/uscw/features/regimental/cavalry.cfm

Schiller, G. The Japanese sword law. Available at: http://www.una.edu/faculty/takeuchi/DrT_Jpn_Culture_files/Nihon_to_files/SwordLawLetter.htm

Suino, N. (2001). *The art of Japanese swordsmanship: A manual of Eishin-ryu Iaido*. NY: Weatherhill Publishing.

United States Code, (1966). Volume 16, United States Code Section 470.

Wikipedia (n.d.). List of National Treasures of Japan available at: http://en.wikipedia.org/wiki/List_of_National_Treasures_of_Japan_%28crafts-swords%29 (Translated list available from the ACA's database, available at: http://www.bunka.go.jp/bsys/index.asp)

Yoshihara, Y. (1987). *The craft of the Japanese sword*. New York: Kondasha International.

Yumoto, J. (1997). *The samurai sword*. Tokyo: Charles E. Tuttle Publishing.

Oshigata:
Appreciating Japanese Sword Tracings for Their Reference and Beauty
by Anthony DiCristofano

Illustration courtesy of Dreamstime.com

Oshigata are full-length and full-size tracings or rubbings of Japanese swords, and have been used for hundreds of years to establish detailed records and references of individual Japanese swords. The word *oshigata*, when written in Japanese, is made up of two kanji characters. The first character is *osu* (押), meaning to push or to press; the second character is *kata* (型), meaning to model, mold, style, or shape. When the two characters are combined, phonetic changes occur and the pronunciation becomes oshigata.

There are three main forms of sword oshigata: full-length oshigata, partial oshigata of a portion of the sword, and oshigata of the tang (*nakago*) of the sword. A full-length oshigata depicts the entire sword and tang. A partial oshigata can display the tang and the tip or point (*kissaki*), along with the *monouchi* area (approximately the first thirty centimeters down from the point). A tang oshigata focuses on the tang and is intended to illustrate the details of the tang alone.

In modern times there are some highly skilled, specialized photographers who can capture most of the finer details present in Japanese swords. However, there are always certain facets or details of the sword that elude the camera's eye. A well-drawn oshigata may show the aspects that are especially difficult to capture with photography. Among these are *hataraki*, characteristic details or features that appear along and inside of the *hamon* (hardened edge of the sword). In general, these complex and important details do not show up at all, or only show up very poorly or incompletely in photographs. When making an oshigata, the hamon and inclusive features are carefully scrutinized and meticulously drawn in by hand in order to record every detail and nuance present in the blade itself. These specific details are unique, distinctive characteristics of individual swords. Well-drawn oshigata can often be used to identify specific swords hundreds of years after an oshigata has been made. Today, probably the best way to completely display a Japanese sword in print and allow people to study and examine all of its critical details is to present a full-size oshigata along with an identically sized photograph side by side.

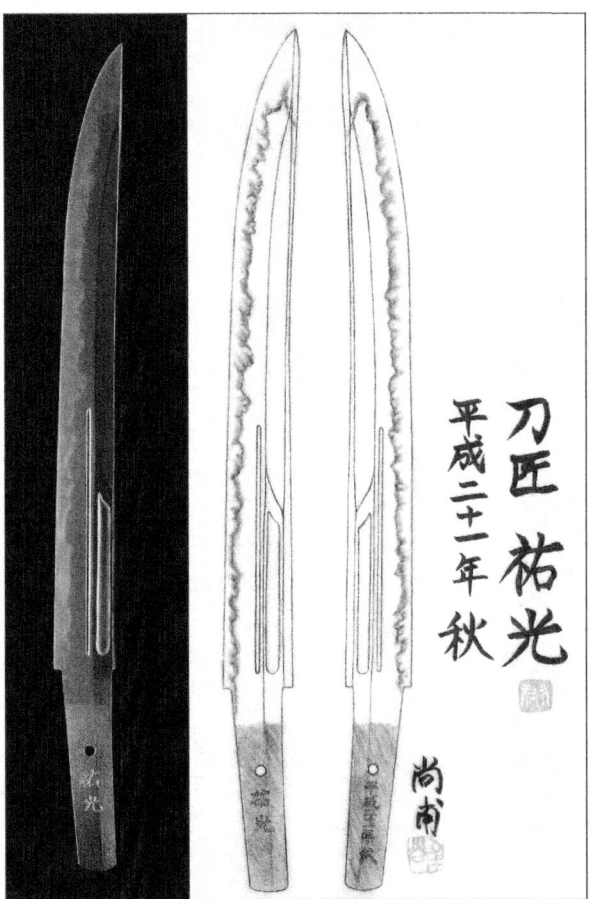

Figure 1: A traditional Japanese sword (*kanmuri otoshi wakizashi*) by the author and signed "Sukemitsu" (Anthony DiCristofano). This sword features halberd-style grooves (*naginata hi*) and an irregular clove-shaped temper line (*chōji midare hamon*). Naganata hi are a characteristic group of grooves and bevels on a blade as seen here. Images copyright by A. DiChristofano.

The Process

Making an oshigata requires skill, time, and great patience. One must have a steady hand and a keen eye for details. Furthermore, creating an oshigata comes with a burden of responsibility in trying to depict the details of an individual sword as accurately as possible. The main material and tools used to make an oshigata are a fibrous or thin, textured Japanese paper, a form of dried ink called *sekkaboku* used in a block or pucklike shape, and sketching pencils. There are various methods to steady or stabilize the paper covering the sword during the process because any movement can result in distortions and deviations in the oshigata from the actual shape of the sword. The main outline of the sword and the tang, along with details (in relief) on the sword, such as *hi* (grooves) and *horimono* (decorative engravings), are produced by rubbing the sekkaboku on the paper, which is placed over the blade. This can prove to be a difficult task, as just the right amount of pressure and rubbing will be necessary to clearly produce integral details in addition to the overall shape without damaging the paper. Once this stage is completed, the hamon and all of its fine details and distinguishing features must be painstakingly drawn in, inch by inch.

Oshigata must depict important details of the sword in order to permit a close examination and study of the sword:

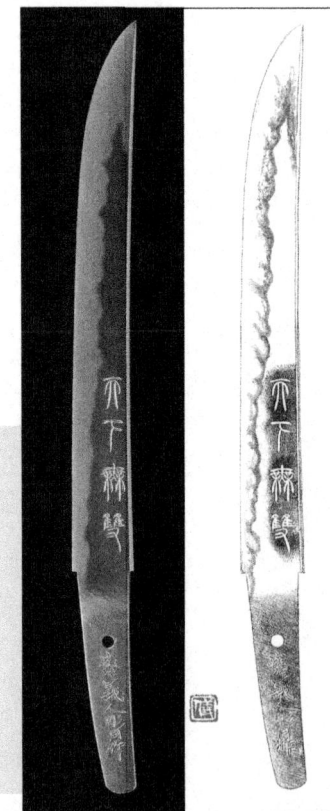

- *hamon* (刃文 hardened portion of the blade along the cutting edge)
- *hi* (grooves)
- *horimono* (彫り物 carvings)
- *nakago* (tang)
- *sugata* (姿 shape)

Figure 2: A flat surface blade without ridges (*hira-zukuri tanto*) made by Yoshindo Yoshihara. This tanto has engravings (*horimono*) and a *saka choji* temper pattern ("saka" means that the clove-shaped waves are all slanted in one direction and are not perpendicular to the edge of the blade).

Copyright by A. DiChristofano.

DISCERNIBLE FEATURES

Overall Sword Shape

The *sugata* is the overall shape of the sword. The sugata has changed over the years, reflecting the influence of evolving methods of warfare and other factors. The influence of specific swordsmiths and schools can also be a factor affecting the sugata. In addition, repeated polishing or repairs over centuries can alter or erode the shape of a sword.

The sugata must be shown with a full-length oshigata. Consequently, this makes a full-length oshigata my favorite and preferred type of oshigata. Some of the main features displayed by a full-length oshigata will include the amount of curvature (*sori*), the center and variation of the sori, the amount of taper in the blade, the shape of the point (*kissaki*), and the shape of the tang.

Hamon

For well over twelve hundred years, Japanese swordsmiths have employed special methods to differentially heat treat a blade, and this results in a hardened edge on the sword, allowing it to take on a very sharp edge, while simultaneously allowing the back or spine of the blade to remain ductile and resilient. This process creates a visible difference in the structure of the steel between the body and edge of the sword. The visible hardened area along the edge is referred to as the *hamon*. Examining a well-drawn oshigata will permit close examination of the hamon. Initially it will provide an indication of the style or type of hamon: for example straight, semicircular waves, or clove-shaped waves, just to name a few. Other features of the hamon's shape, such as the start of the hamon at the base of the blade (*yakidashi*) and the hardened area within the point at the tip of the sword (*boshi*), will also be evident in the oshigata. Another prominent characteristic in which a well-drawn oshigata excels is its ability to clearly display the details of the *hataraki* within the hamon. Many variations escape photography, or even the human eye, in the absence of proper lighting and inspection angles. These variations include lines extending down into the hardened edge (*ashi*), a double-lined hamon, and a partially disconnected ashi pattern that appears as spots within the hamon.

Tang

Much can be learned about a Japanese sword by studying the tang. Careful scrutiny of the tang is an important part of sword appraisal. Beyond illustrating the main shape and the characteristics of the tang, such as the length, width, taper, and style of the tang's end or tip, an oshigata will display additional key features, including the chiseled signature, style of file marks, hole for retention peg, and other elements.

Groves and Carvings

Any grooves or carvings present on the sword will be portrayed in the oshigata as well. The various types of hi and the method in which the grooves end will be indicated in the oshigata. Carvings on Japanese swords are quite different from western-style engravings in that they can have much more relief and a three-dimensional character. This relief is brought out by the careful rubbing process involved in producing the oshigata, allowing for an accurate representation that can be used for study and reference.

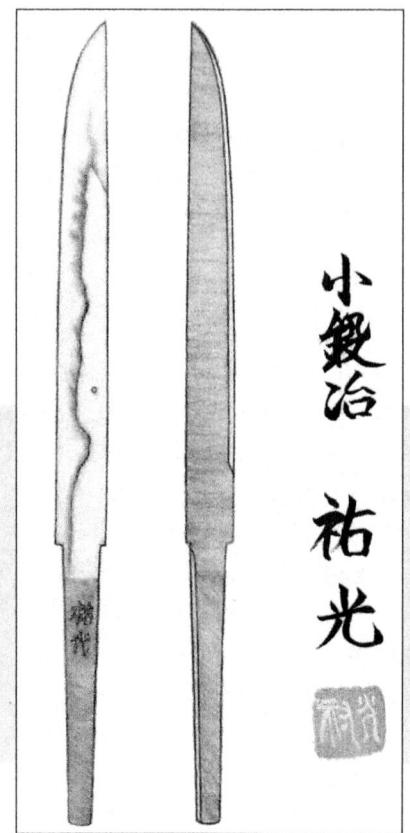

Figure 3:
A *kogatana* is a small utility blade or knife made in the same manner as a sword. This one was made by the author and signed "Sukemitsu" (Anthony DiCristofano). The kogatana has a temper pattern that is shaped to depict Mt. Fuji and the moon.

Copyright by A. DiChristofano.

Final View

Modern and skillfully done sword photography can show much of a sword's character and detail. Although photographs provide for enjoyable viewing, there is no substitute for having a blade in hand for examination and study. I must admit that there is something uniquely satisfying in being able to view the essential details of a sword in the form of an oshigata.

Bladed Weaponry with Illustrations from the Japanese Antique Sword Museum
by Harunaka Hoshino

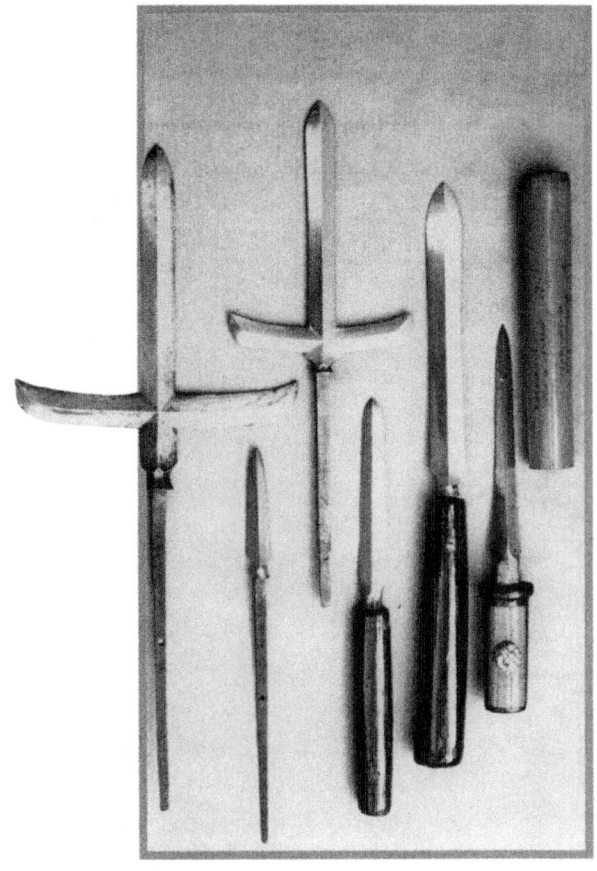

Various *yari* (spears).

For Japan, the sword has been the symbol of martial strength and beauty. Its history of over 1700 years continues to influence Japan's modern swordmaking, and is presented in museums and books enjoyed throughout the world. Bladed weapons have always been held in the highest respect by the Japanese. The samurai sword or *katana* is representative of all Japanese bladed weaponry.

Although structure, size and technique may vary, it is the predecessor from which all other Japanese blades were derived. Initially, the Chinese-style twin-bladed straight swords, called *jian* in Mandarin, were imported. These swords as made by Korean and Chinese swordsmiths were so thin that when held parallel to the ground they bent from their own weight. Because they were not well made and often broke, they were used primarily for ceremonial purposes.

Chinese swordsmiths (*Kara-kanuchi*)
Korean swordsmiths (*Aya-kanuchi*)
Japanese swordsmiths (*Yamato-kanuchi*)

The folding, forging and tempering processes of steel-making were introduced by Japanese swordsmiths between the third and fourth centuries. A tempering process was added as a means of generating curvature (*sori*). Curvature also lessened the chances for problems that were common in maneuvering the straight sword—the severance of one's foot or, when mounted, a horse's ear, etc.

Technically, there are two major categories of bladed weaponry: straight (*chokuto*) and curved (*wanto*). Within the straight blade category is the double-bladed straight sword (*tsurugi*), ninja sword (*ninjato*), large ninja sword (*dai ninjato*), spear (*yari*), and dagger (*tanto* and *kaito*). The curved category includes the long sword with deep curvature (*tachi*), the regular sword (*katana*), the Japanese halberd (*naginata*), and some specialized daggers. Some weapons, such as kaito or kaiken, may fall into either the straight or curved categories. While all were "edged" and/or "pointed," each weapon's characteristic structure and related applications defined its own unique style of movements for usage.

BASIC CATEGORIES OF JAPANESE BLADED WEAPONRY

Straight Blade (*chukuto*)
- double-bladed straight sword (*tsurugi*)
- Ninja sword (*ninjato*)
- large ninja sword (*dai-ninjato*)
- spear (*yari*)
- dagger (*tanto* and *kaito*)

Curved Blade (*wanto*)
- long sword with deep curvature (*tachi*)
- regular sword (*katana*)
- halberd (*naginata*)
- specialized daggers

Each and every bladed weapon of the Japanese tradition was an inimitable expression of form, artistry, culture and custom. The majority were not a result of mass production. Each component, from the tip to the hilt, was hand-forged by the swordsmiths (*katana-kaji*). While some were expediently made to last a short stint in battle, others required nearly a lifetime to complete to meet the standard of perfection some craftsmen upheld. Knowledge of how to create such weaponry necessitated at least twenty-five years of experience. Complete mastery of usage required even longer. All Japanese bladed weapons are characterized by intricate construction, artistic metalwork, colorful history and proud tradition.

The swordsmith began his meticulous work by melting iron-bearing sand at a temperature between 1,100 and 1,450 degrees Fahrenheit. The iron separated from the sand, forming small steel pellets which bore trace elements of crude carbon and charcoal called *tamahagane*. By reheating the tamahagane, which resulted in the bonding of the pellets, the entire mass was then instantly chilled for a double hardening effect. The steel was then hammered into small coin-like pieces, stacked together, then reheated several more times at 650 degrees Fahrenheit. Each reheating made the bonding more stable and secure. Then, while still hot and pliable, it was strauthed into an elongated shape in preparation for the "folding process." Three different types of steel were formed: soft, medium and hard. A sword's superlative quality required five folds (32 layers) for its soft-steel shock-absorbing qualities, ten folds (1,024 layers) for its medium-steel flexible resiliency and fifteen folds (32,768 layers) for its hardsteel superior cutting ability.

The next step was to undertake the forging process called *kitae*. This involved forging the three types of steel, consistently positioning the hardest type as the cutting edge, to form one solid weapon. After the forging process, yet while the metal was still quite hot, the blade was pounded to its required size and then chilled. To give the sword its cutting ability, a special clay was coated on the surface of the blade, which is a process called *tsuchioki*. Upon an intense reheating followed by immediate immersion in cold water, the clay-laden edge was made harder. This reheating process in called *yaki-ire* and resulted in the tempering line (*hamon*) and the curvature (*sori*).

FOLDING PROCESS (*orikawshi*)

Fold(s)	Layers	Fold(s)	Layers
1	2	11	2,048
2	4	12	4,096
3	8	13	8,192
4	16	14	16,384
5	32	15	32,768
6	64	16	65,536
7	128	17	131,072
8	256	18	262,144
9	512	19	524,288
10	1,024	20	1,048,576

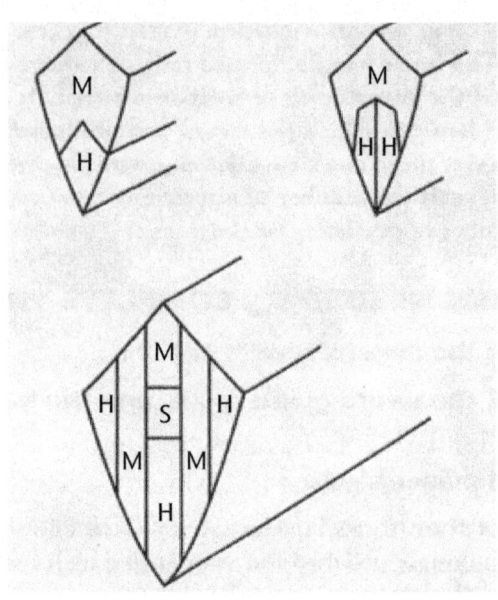

Steel Types	Folds	Layers
soft (S)	5	32
medium (M)	10	1,024
hard (H)	15	32,768

There are mainly two types of tempering lines. One is straight (*sugu-hamon*) and the other is wavy (*notare-hamon*). Three different kinds of curvatures appeared: the equal or even curvature (*kyou-zori*), that which curved more near the tang (*koshi-zori*), and that which curved downward (*saki-zori*). The degree of curvature depended on the reheating temperature and length of immersion time. Those factors were determined by the swordsmiths' training within their respective traditional school.

There are five of these schools (*gokaden*) listed from the oldest to the most recently formed: 1) the Yamato School near Nara, an ancient capital city, 2) the Yamashiro School in Kyoto, the capital before Edo or Tokyo, 3) the Bizen School, now Okayama Prefecture, 4) the Mino School, now Gifu Prefecture, and 5) the Soshu School in Kamakura area, now Kamakura city in Kanagawa prefecture. These five sword-making traditions each manufactured blades with unique markings called *nioi* and *nie*. The nioi and nie result from the tempering process which leaves particular patterns in the blade. Those patterns which resemble clouds or mist of fog are called *nioi*. When large austenite crystal-like dots are visible, the patterns are called nie. This tempering process requires heating at very higher temperatures. All Japanese swords contain both nie and nioi to some degree. However, the Soshu swordsmiths emphasize strong nie (*ara-nie*); the Yamato swordsmiths are characterized by moderate nie (*chu-nie*); the Bizen swordsmiths by abundant nioi (*hon-nioi*); and the Mino swordsmiths, primarily by nioi.

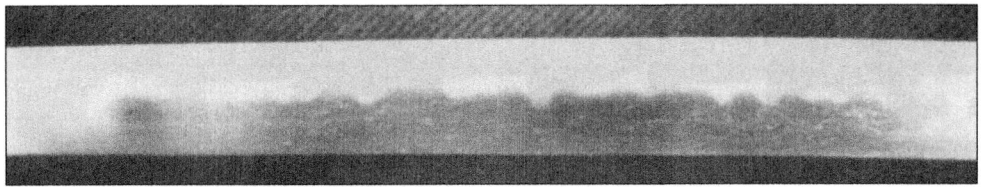

Tempering line (*hamon*).

FINAL STAGES OF SWORDSMITHING
- adjusting the curvature (*sorinaoshi*)
- rough polishing (*kaji-togi*)
- carving the decorative grooves (*horimono-ire*)
  Grooves on the katana's blade were designed to lessen the weapon's overall weight by five to twenty percent. Contrary to popular belief, these indentations were not intended for blood drainage.
- filing the tang which includes inscribing the signature (*mei-ire*).
  The inner handle, termed *tang* or *nakago*, displays the signature of the swordsmith or weapon's owner. It also designates the area of Japan in which the sword was produced. Similar to the serial number, these mark each katana with its own identity. The tang also reveals the number of alterations a sword had gone through by the number of peg-holes (*mekugi-ana*) it exhibits.

CRAFTSMEN NEEDED TO COMPLETE THE SWORD
- Master of the metal sleeve (*habaki-shi*)
- Master of the sword guard (*tsuba*) and the handle ornament (*kinkou-shi*)
- Scabbard maker (*saya-shi*)
- Sword polisher (*togi-shi*), who corrected the minor flaws of the sword, then painstakingly polished the swords to a high luster by the skilled application of twenty-one specialized types of grinding stones.

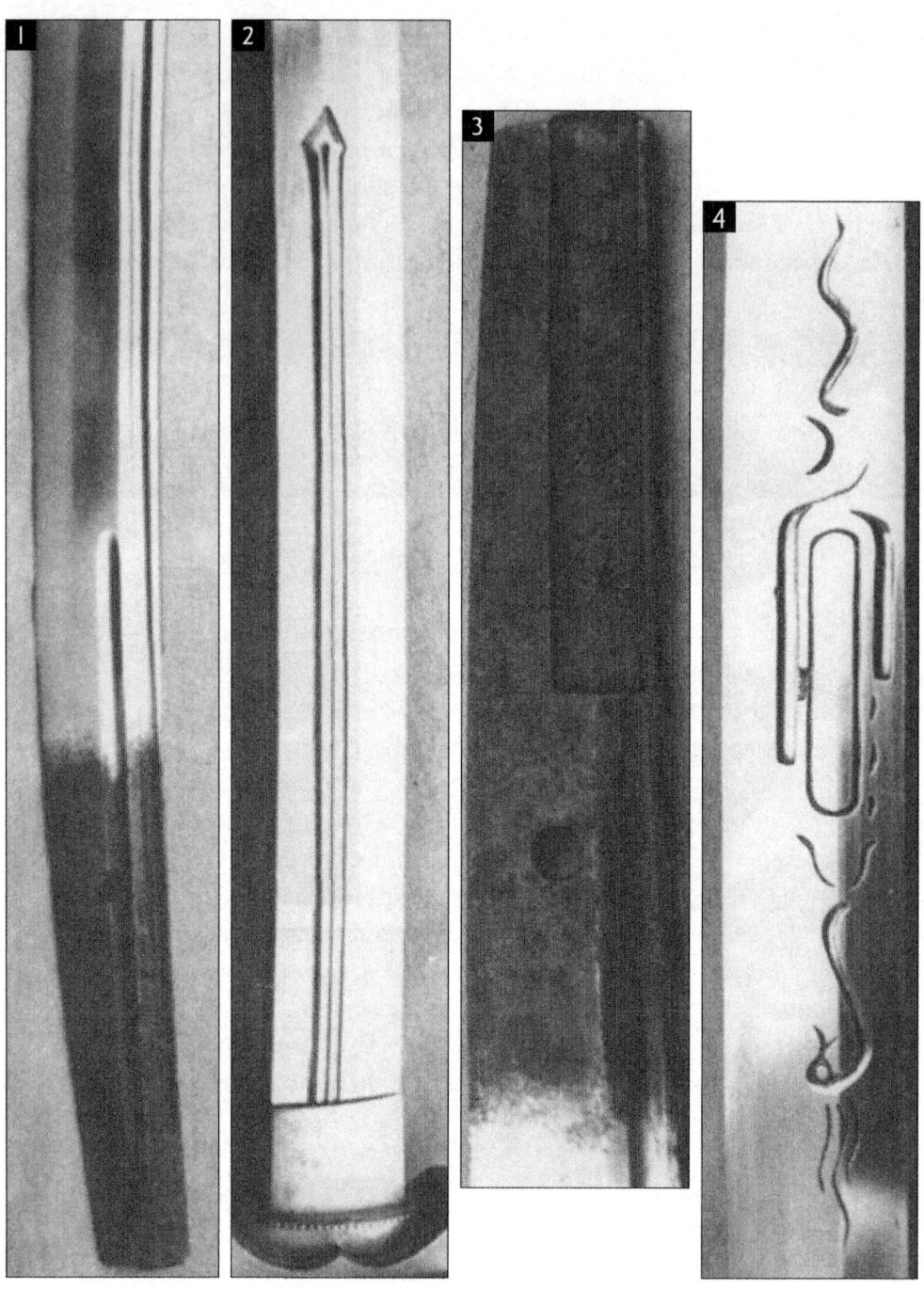

1) a 380-year-old sword with grooves (*hi*).
2) a straight sword (*suken*) engraved on the blade.
3) a folded inscription (*orikaeshi-mei*) by Ietsugu, a seventeenth century swordsmith.
4) a dragon (*kurika*) engraved on a blade, symbolizing the powers of an almighty deity.

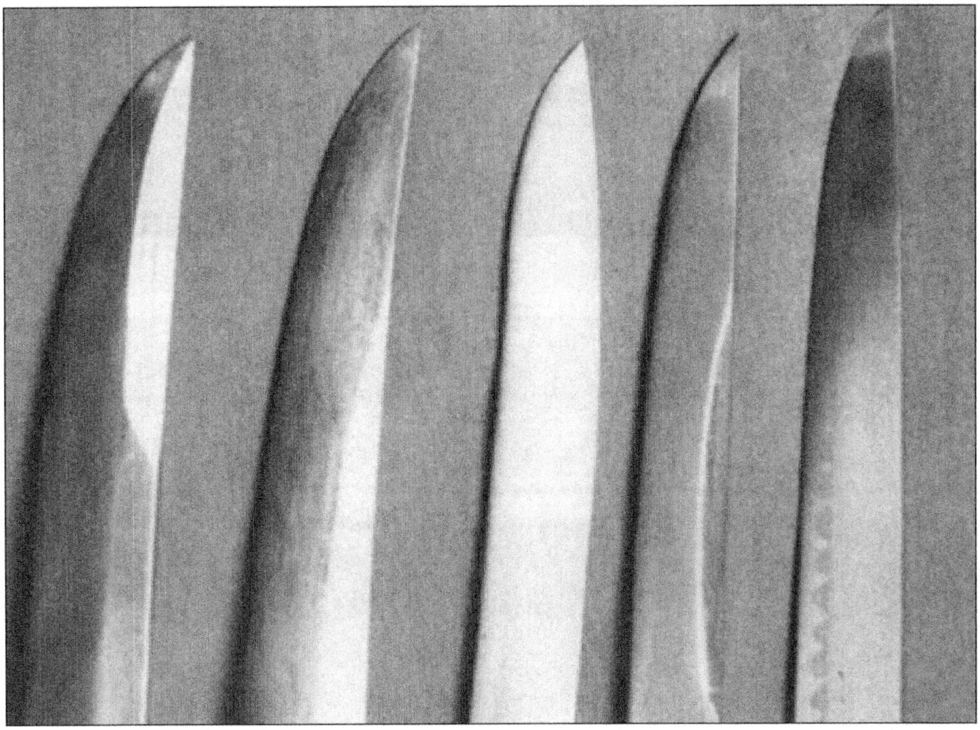

Assortment of sword tips and guards (*tsuba*).

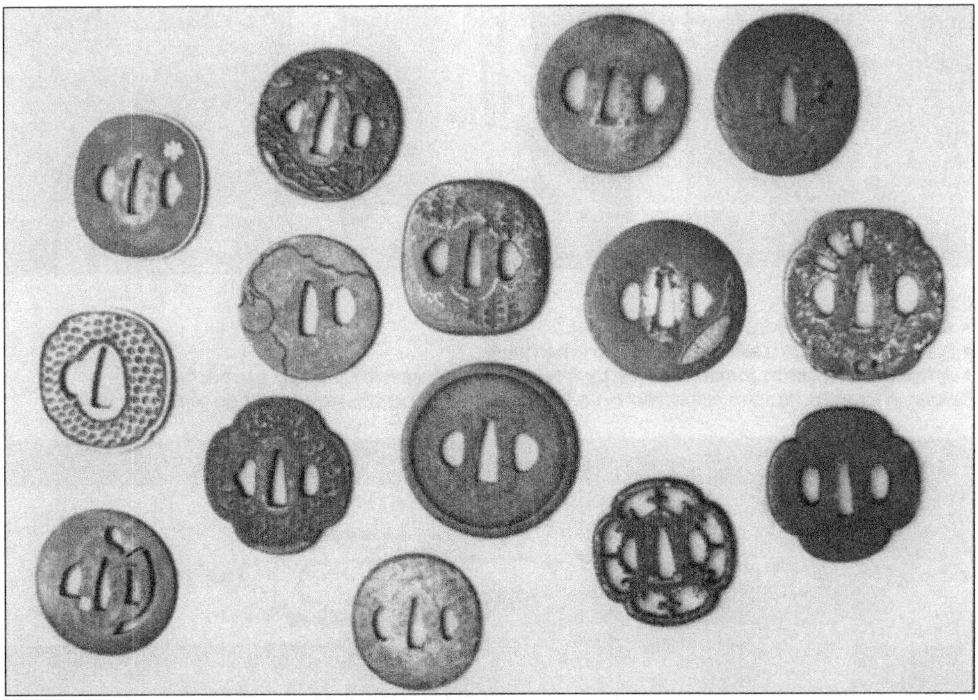

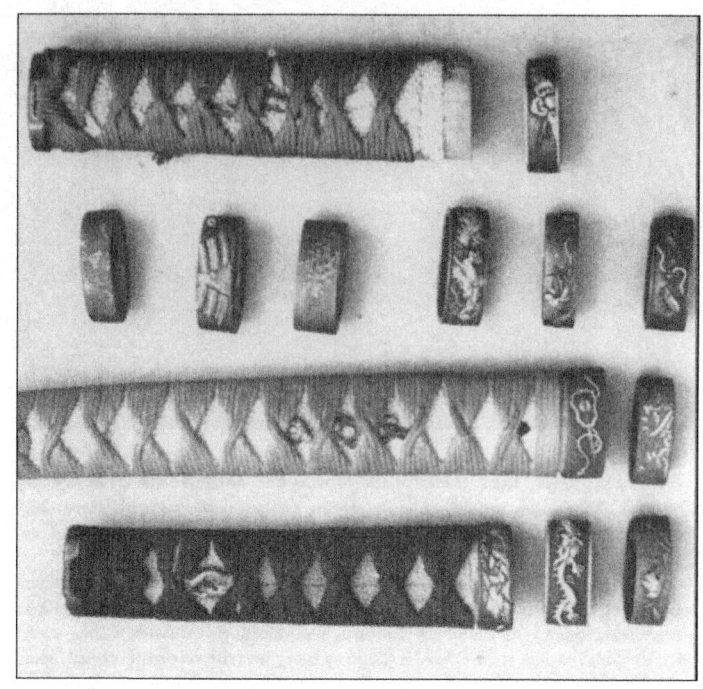

Sword handle (*tsuka*) including the metal tips called *fuchigane*.
Below: Ornaments (*menuki*) which are located on the handle.

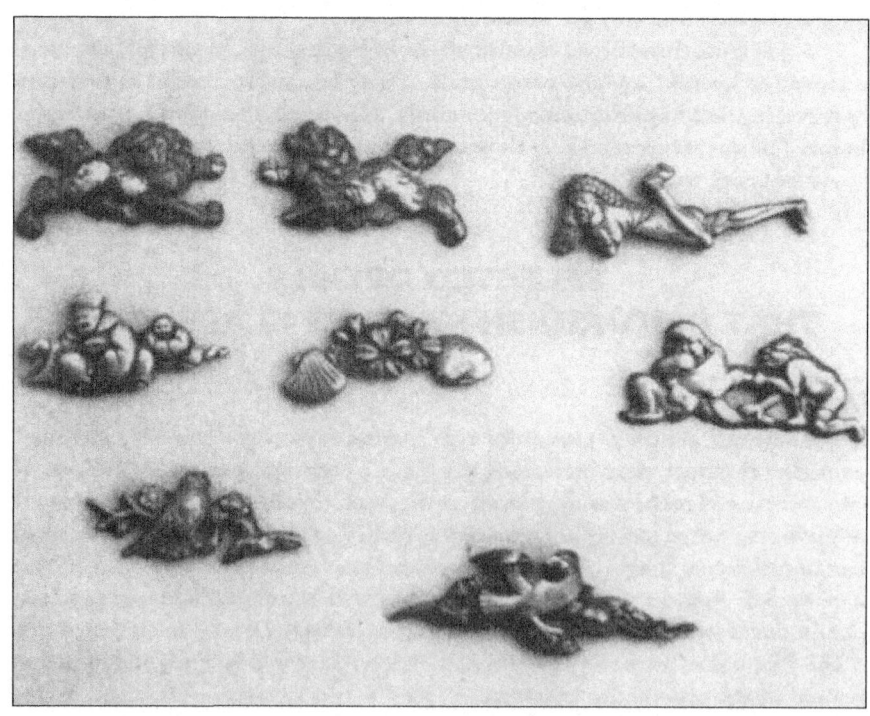

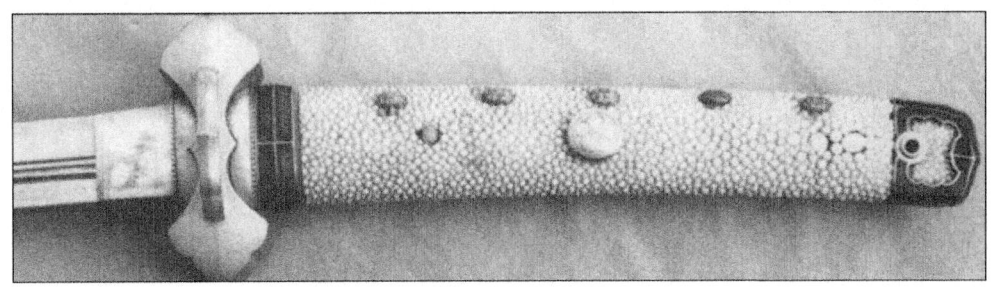

Detail of a feudal warlord's tachi. The blade is approximately 500 years old, while the dressing or fittings (*koshiraewere*) were produced in 1790.

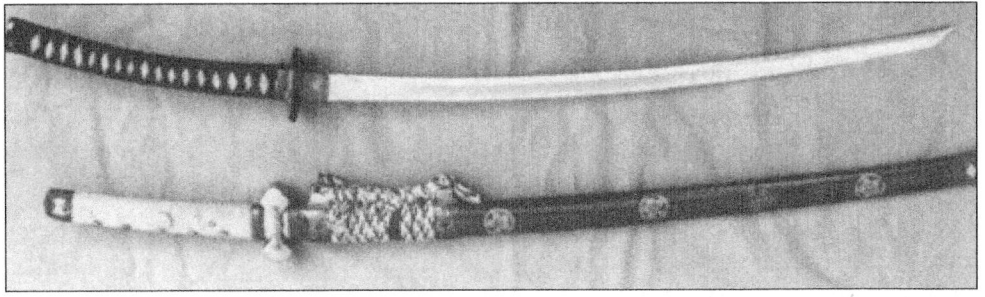

A feudal warlord's long sword (*Daimyo-tachi*) and the 750-year-old Efu-tachi with detailed handle shown above.

There are five basic grades of sword weapons. Within each grade are subdivisions. The major groupings are superior quality (*saijou-saku*), above high grade (*joujou-saku*), high grade (*jou-saku*), above middle grade (*chujou-saku*), and middle grade (*chu-saku*).

All bladed weaponry can also be categorized in five distinct classifications: long, short, twin, flexible and equipment-type. The spear (*yari*), Japanese halberd (*naginata*), extra long tachi (*oh-danbira*, *seoi-dachi*, or *no-dachi*), long sword with deep curvature (*tachi*) are in the long category; the sword (*katana*), short sword (*wakizashi* or *shouto*), fixed naginata often shortened at the tang (*naginatanaoshi*), ninja sword (*ninja-to*) and large ninja sword (*dai-ninja-to*) are in the mid-length category; and the dagger (*tanto* or *kaito*), concealed daggers (*kakushi-tanto* and *kakushi-kaito*) are in the short category.

Aside from these broad classifications of blade shape, blade tips, referred to as *kissaki* or *kirisaki*, are also categorized. It may be almost straight in preference for thrusting techniques or, more commonly, substantially curved for cutting and slicing. The curvature increases the ease and speed with which cutting and slicing movements are made.

Selected Details That Distinguish Various Blade Types

Tachi

In the seventh century, curvature was incorporated into Japanese swords by tempering the steel, thus increasing the blade's cutting capacity. As a result, the long and curved tachi was developed as the ancestor of the katana. Because the Mongols attempted to invade Japan twice, in 1274 and 1278, many swordsmiths started producing longer, larger, thicker and heavier tachi-styled blades. Thus, huge swords such as the author's *no-dachi* (field-bandit tachi) were produced. The no-dachi was used for cutting off the front leg of the horses in the battlefields of the Nanbokucho Era (1334–1389). Later, in the Edo Era, it became the weapon of the official decapitators.

Uchigatana

Japan's civil wars of the Azuchi-Momoyama Era led to the development of the uchi-gatana, which could be worn cutting-edge up at the soldier's waist so as to combine drawing and cutting actions with one hand in a single strike. The uchi-gatana was more or less twenty-four inches in length and well-made for the close-range combat in the battlefield. The uchi-gatana is a member of the same family as the tachi and katana; it has the curvature of the tachi sword and the durability of the katana sword.

Katana

The katana was considered the ultimate achievement within the menagerie of Japanese bladed weaponry. Historically, the creation of Japanese weaponry began close to 3,000 years ago. This date correlates with the Japanese people's settlement of Japan. The first weapons were made entirely of stone and were employed mainly for hunting. Their defensive use was but a secondary consideration. The Kamakura, Nanbokucho and Momoyama eras witnessed many wars. These relentless campaigns promoted many military improvements, such as lighter katana and protective equipment, which could be worn for long hours without hindering a soldier's speed or power. In addition to established thrusting techniques, defensive blocks, cutting and slicing movements were accepted as standard katana usage (see illustrations near the end of this chapter).

Tanto, Kaito, Kaiken, Futokoro-gatana

History does not record when the first tanto dagger was actually created. It is known, however, that the tousu-type dagger appeared in the eighth century during the Nara Era (708–781). Its entire length was six to eight inches. It had a wooden handle shaped like an elongated "V" and was used both as a utility knife and for assassination.

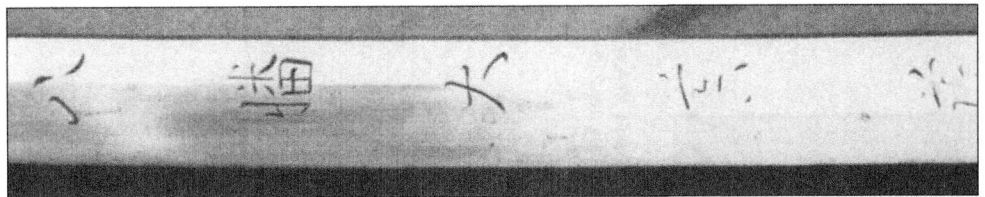

A religious chant (*hachi-man-dai-bo-satsu*) engraved on the blade of a 500-year-old tachi.

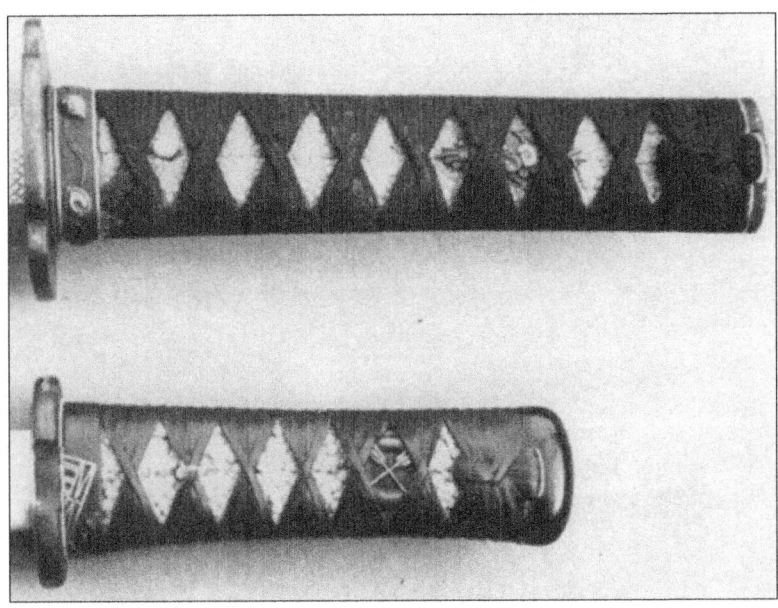

Shown above is a mid-sized sword (*wakizashi*) handle compared with a dagger (*tanto*) handle shown below.

Kinds of tanto extant from the Kamakura Era (1182-1333):
- cormorant bird neck shape (*u-no-kubi-zukuri*)
- a large tip or small tip and a straight blade (*kanmuri-otoshi-zukuri*)
- flat shape (*hira-zukuri*)
- one-sided flat shape (*kata-kiriha-zukuri*)
- double-bladed dagger (*ryouba-zukuri*)
- two marked mid-lines (*shinogi-zukuri*)

Three main shapes of tanto:
- straight or non-curved blade (*chokuto* or *muzori*)
- upward curved dagger (*saki-zori tanto*)
- downward curved dagger (*takenoku-zori* or *saki-zori*)

Two special types of tanto:
- armor-piercing (yoroi-doushi)
- *Kaito* or *kaiken* "concealable" armor-piercing tanto were used on the battlefield. They were usually double-bladed, which made them doubly dangerous. Double-bladed weapons have the advantage of making a larger wound than single-bladed weapons and thereby causing more severe injury. Kaito or kaiken were shorter than other tanto. They were, therefore, easily concealed under the arm or within a kimono sleeve.

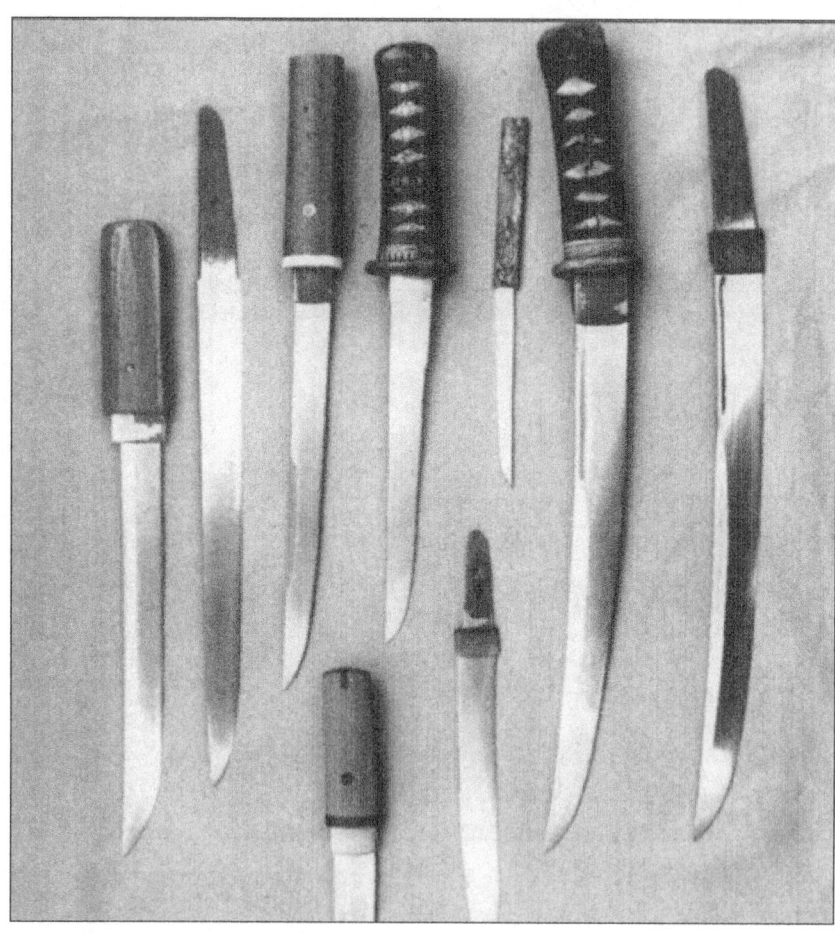

A display showing a variety of tanto types.

A tanto produced by Sagami-no-Kami Masatsune in August, 1593. At the top are a gasket (*seppa*), metal sleeve (*habaki*), guard (*tsuba*), and another gasket. Below the handle is a scabbard (*saya*).

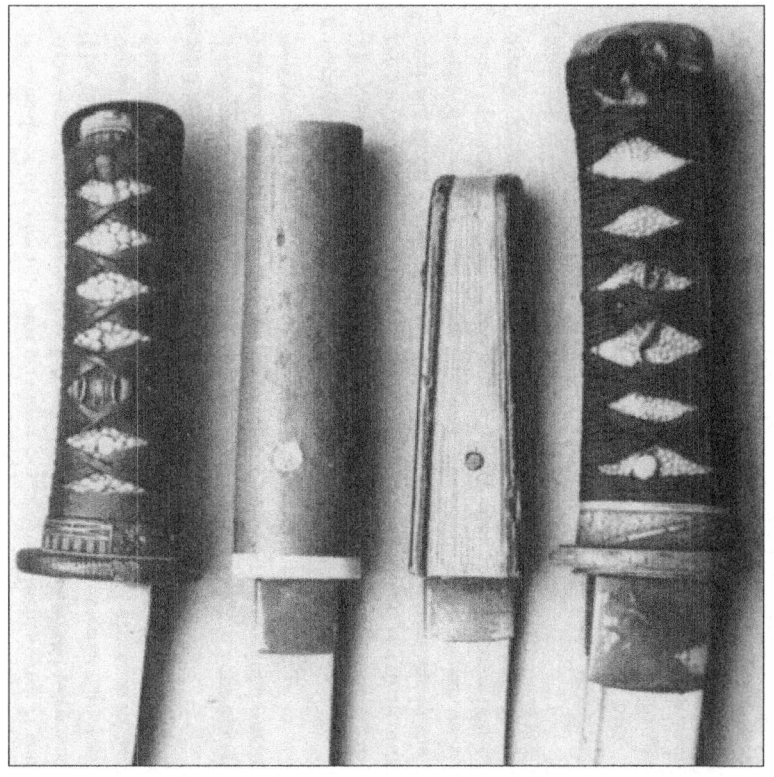

An assortment of tanto handles. The two shown in the middle are armor-piercing daggers (*yoroidoushi*) with blade tips tapered for their particular usage.

The Katana's Companion Sword (*wakizashi*)

The wakizashi is between twelve and twenty-three inches long. There are three categories of wakizashi blades: large (*dai*), medium (*chu*), and small (*shou*). Technically, the wakizashi blades never existed before the Azuchi-Momoyama Era (1573–1623). The author discovered a wakizashi with the signature of Sanjou Munechika in San Francisco, California in 1984. However, the swordsmith Sanjou Munechika produced only tachi swords, naginata blades and yari spears nearly one thousand years ago. Therefore, the wakizashi blade inspected by the author was without question *agimei* (fake signature). Wakizashi is similar to the shouto of the samurai's dai-shou pair of blades; however, it was worn alone by the townsmen (gangsters, merchants and craftsmen) with the permission of the Tokugawa Shogunate in the Edo Era. The fittings (*koshirae*) of the townsmen's sword were usually more valuable than the blade itself. The wakizashi was also used as the katana by the young samurai who could not handle the standard-size katana.

Spears (yari)

Most yari tips were nearly rectangular and two-dimensional. Others were flatter between their cutting edges. Its steel blade normally ranged from three to twelve inches in length, undergoing the identical forging, folding, bonding and tempering processes as the katana (for illustrations of various spear types, see page 92).

Four types of yari:
- straight spears (*jiki-yari* or *sugu-yari*)
  The blade of the ohmi-no yari was over twenty-four inches long. It was used for executions as well as for ornamental and ceremonial purposes. The third longest spear in the world, as confirmed by extensive international research, is in our own Japanese Antique Sword Museum in San Francisco. It is thirty-five inches long.
- hooked spears (*kama-yari*)
  There are two types of hooked spears: 1) the single-hooked kata-kamayari and 2) the double-hooked jumonji-yari. Hooks were designed simply to prevent deeper penetration upon impalement.
- socket spears (*fukuro yari*)
  The socket spear was created in Fukuoka Prefecture located in the northern part of Kyushu Island. The steel portion of the Fukuro yari fit directly over the shaft. This increased the weapon's strength, especially in the upper area used for deflective blocking. The result was a greater resistance to cracks, splits and breaks, which were often the outcome of direct attacks upon the wooden shaft.

- **Kikuchi family spears** (*Kikuchi-yari*)

  The Kikuchi-yari was the crowning achievement of spear development. It was so valued as to be referred to as "Kikuchi," the surname of its creator. The blade of the Kikuchi-yari was actually an elongated dagger (*tanto*) with a tang (*nakago*) of the same length. The Kikuchi-yari's blade and tang are each more or less fourteen inches long. Many Kikuchi-yari were later shortened and altered at the tang. The original tang was simply too long to mount the regular tanto fittings.

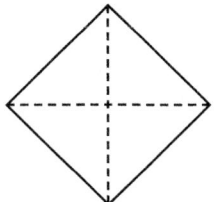  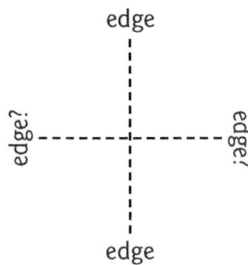

Looking down the central axis of a spear tip. The dimensions from the central axis vary.

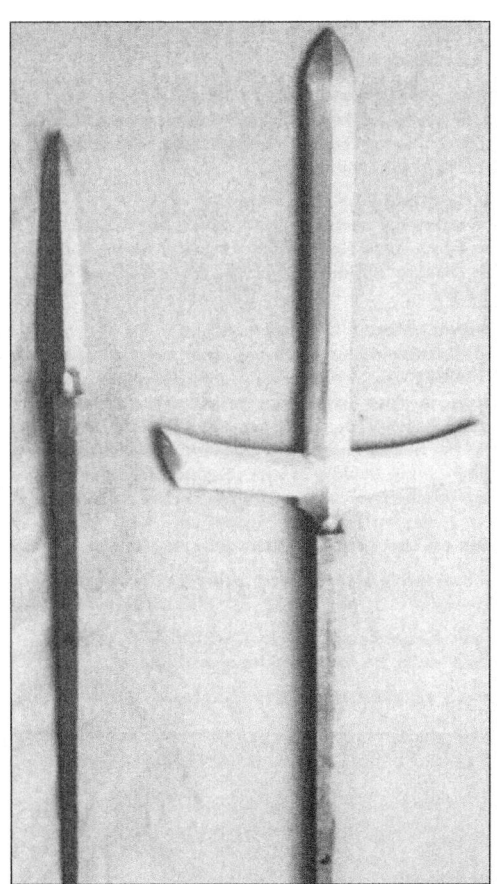 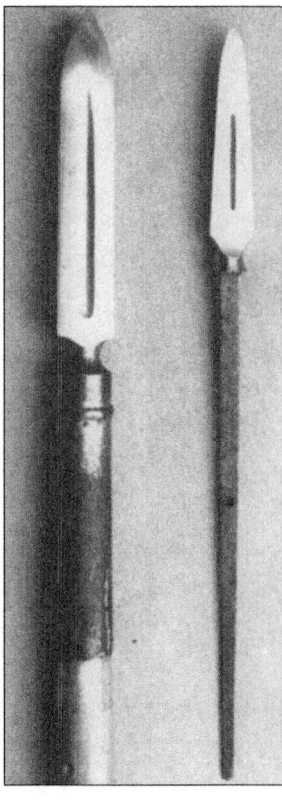

Spear (*yari*) tips. A regular spear made by Aizu-Shimosaka about 300 years ago. The cross-shaped spear (*jumonji-yari*) is approximately 500 years old. A socket spear (*fukuro-yari*), followed by another regular spear by Aizu-Shimosaka.

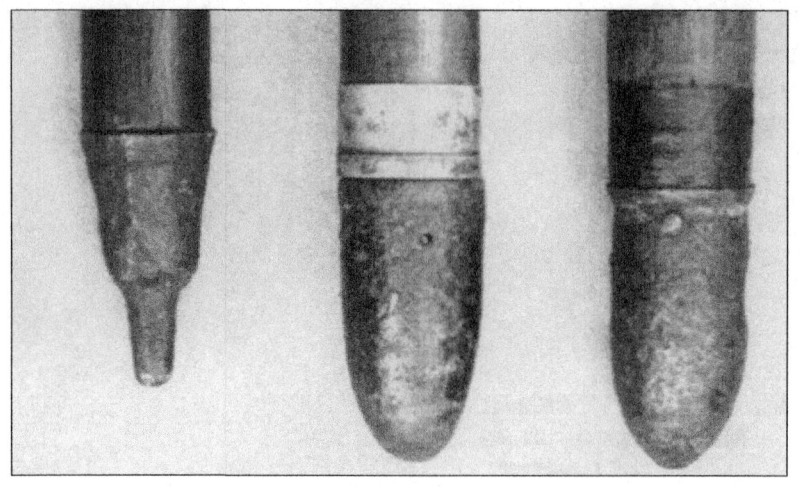

Metal ends (*ishizuki*) for yari.

JAPANESE HALBERD (*naginata*)

Three types of naginata:
- **cormorant bird neck shaped halberd** (*u-no-kubi naginata*)
  This halberd is the product of the Kamakura, Nanbokucho, and Muromachi Eras. The standard u-no-kubi naginata has a short, wide blade with a tang (*nakago*) longer in length than its blade.
- **long bladed naginata** (*nagamaki naginata*)
  This ancient weapon was created and used during the Heian Era (782–1182). It has a long, narrow blade, matched by a thin, elongated nakago. The nagamaki naginata's blade is similar to a iris-leaf shaped blade (*shoubu-zukuri katant*).
- **uniquely shaped halbred** (*tsukushi naginata*)
  This naginata is similar in form and manufacture to a traditional battle ax minus the latter's characteristic spike. Whereas the shafts of the u-nokubi naginata and nagamaki naginata were drilled, these blades were inserted into the handle's shaft, then secured by a peg. The unsharpened edge (*mune*) of the tsukushi naginata's blade had a specialized outer attachment. This hollow housing fit over the shaft like a nut and bolt fixture, leaving the edge freely exposed for its effective use as a weapon.

Three theories on the origin of tsukushi naginata:
- The original conception of the weapon occurred before or during the Heian Era.
- The weapon was designed during the Nanbokucho Era (also called the Yoshino Era) and the Muromachi Era.
- It was a relatively modern creation of the Edo Era.

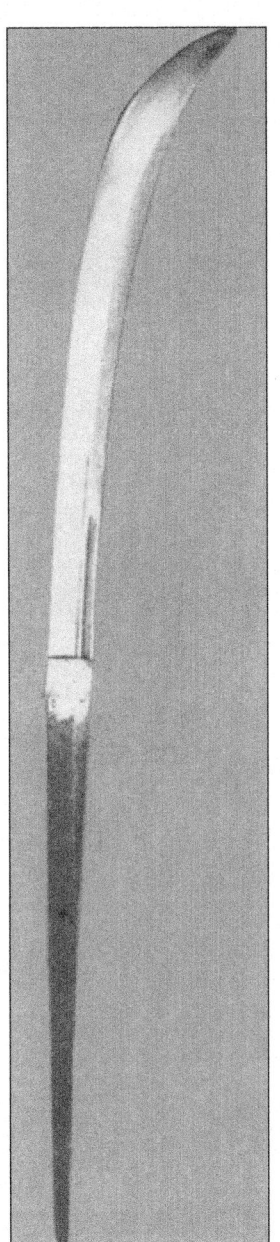

A nagamaki halberd.

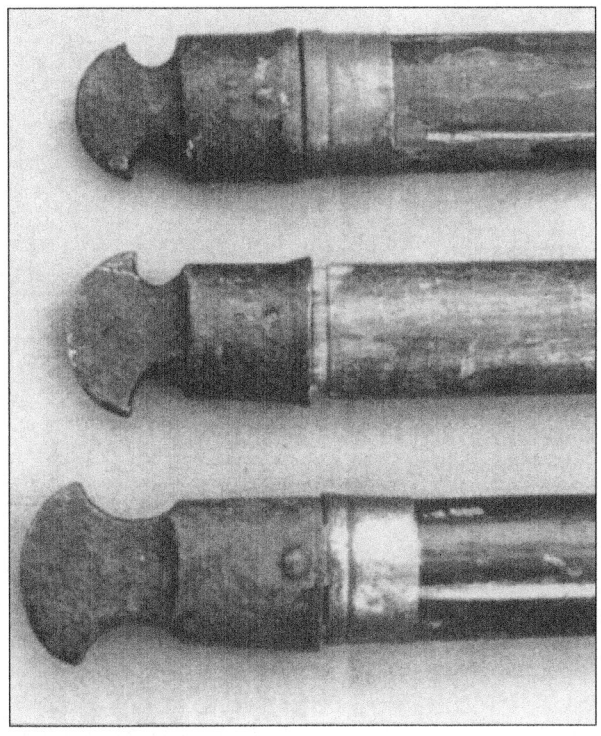

Metal ends (*ishizuki*) for halberds.

MILITARY SWORD (*gunto*)

Two main types of military swords:
- **Kaigunto** – Navy sword characterized by a dark, smooth sharkskin scabbard with two metal loops to attach to the soldier's waist.
- **Rikugunto** – Army sword characterized by an olive drab metal scabbard and one metal loop.

Seven blade types categorized according to periods:
- Koto – old swords produced prior to 1596.
- Shinto – new swords produced between 1596 and 1764.
- Shin-shinto – new swords produced between 1764 and 1867.
- Gendaito – modern swords produced from 1868 and 1944.
- Shouwa-to – Shouwa Era swords produced from 1926 and 1944.
- Shikyu-hin – swords provided for the Japanese Imperial Army or Navy and produced during World War II.

Two kinds of Japanese Government-issue swords (shikyu-hin):
- Kikai-zukuri – swords made by machines. The tempering line is drawn and the blades are oil-cooled.
- Han-kitae-zukuri – swords made 50% by machine and 50% by hand forging. The tempering line is drawn and the blades are oil-cooled or water-cooled.

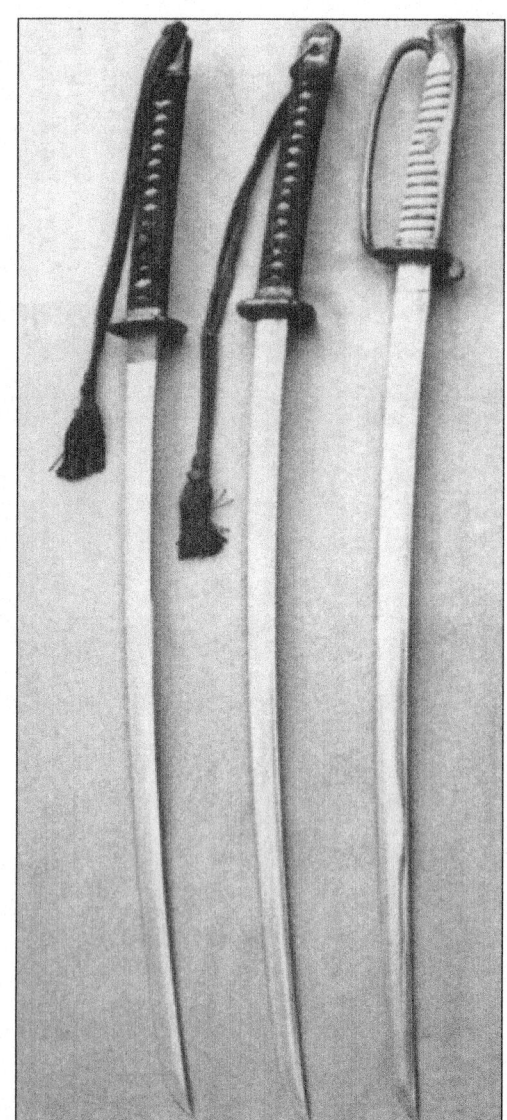

Military Swords (*gunto*):
Left: a katana produced in 1930.
Middle: a katana produced in 1942.
Right: a katana produced in approximately 1600; the dressing (*koshirae*) was made in 1903.

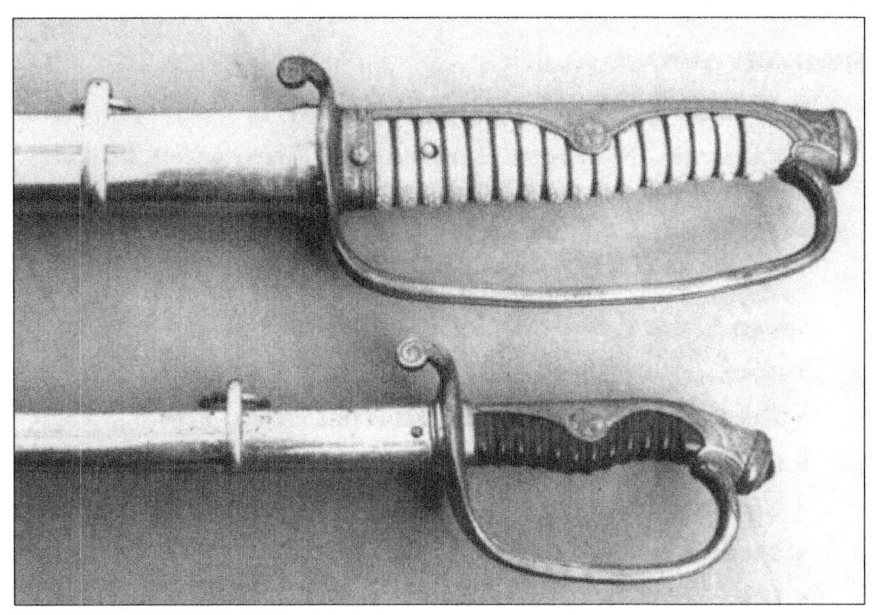

Military sword (*gunto*) handles made in 1903
which were used during the Russo-Japanese War.

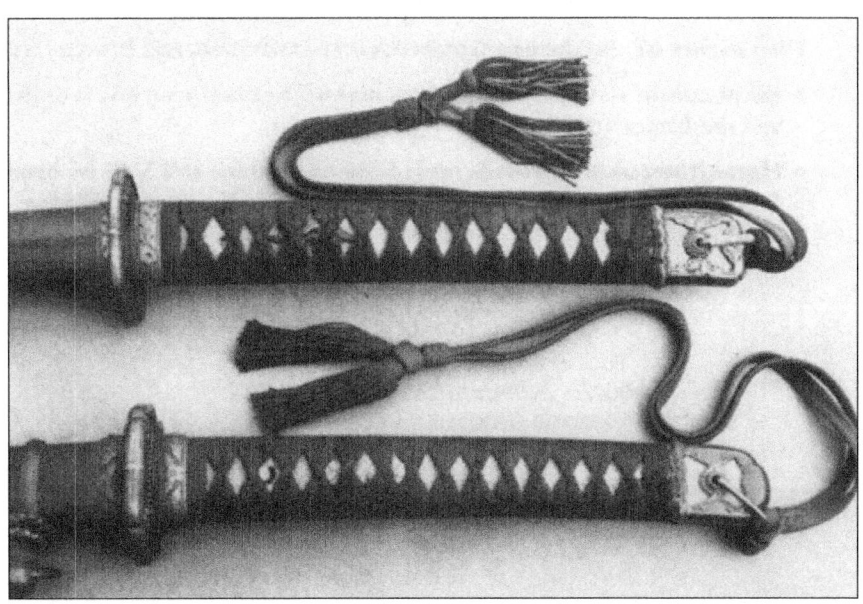

Military sword handles which were used during World War II.

Contact

Mr. Hashino welcomes contact by anyone interested in the museum collection or in receiving information concerning the San Francisco Sword Society or the Japanese Sword Preservation Center. Mr. Harunaka Hoshino, Japanese Antique Sword Museum, P.O. Box 12235, San Francisco, CA 94112. Tel: (415) 334-7260

References

Warner, G., & Draeger, D. (1986). *Japanese swordsmanship: Technique and practice.* Tokyo: Weatherhill.

Kapp, L., & Kapp, H. (1987). *The craft of the Japanese sword.* Tokyo: Kodansha International.

Satoh, K. (1986). *The Japanese sword.* Trans. by Joseph Earle. New York: Kodansha International.

Turnbull, S. (1982). *The book of the samurai: The warrior class of Japan.* New York: Gallery Books.

Ratti, O., & Westbrook, A. (1973). *Secrets of the samurai: A survey of the martial arts of feudal Japan.* Rutland, VT: Charles E. Tuttle.

Amateur Saya Craft: Scabbards in the Making
by Richard W. Babin, Ed.D.

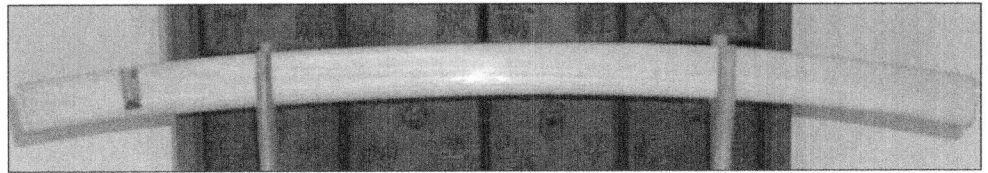

Photographs courtesy of R. Babin.

Introduction*

With care, blades may last forever, but a *saya* (scabbard) should be considered a consumable resource. Just look at the number of blades offered at auction or shows with unserviceable saya. Saya rot, dry out and split, warp, and are broken when stepped or driven upon. They chip and ding easily if dropped or struck, for example, carelessly hitting two saya together. Add to that, the saya split by the poor drawing techniques of beginning iaido or kenjutsu students and the need for a ready source of replacements is obvious. It is often hard to find a stock saya that will fit a given blade, especially without sending a blade to the source with all the inherent risk involved. Custom made saya are expensive and the wait is long, especially if it is for your favorite (or only) *iaito* (practice sword). It is also desirable to have a practice saya for each working sword so that the original saya remains pristine for display or formal purposes.

The present chapter is based on the premise that building a serviceable saya is within the scope and talents of anyone moderately handy with tools. That is not to say that it is easy to produce a fine saya for an art blade. Building a high quality saya requires a fine touch with sharp instruments, extensive experience with carving, an understanding of grain, an excellent sense of proportion and, especially, a good eye for working with curves. However, it is neither difficult nor expensive to build a saya that is moderately attractive and perfectly adequate to either protect a blade or serve during drawing practice with a working blade, either a live blade or a practice blade. Furthermore, this can be done with materials that are easy to obtain and work with. While the use of power tools speeds up the process considerably, they are not critical to the end result.

---

* **Note:** Please refer to glossary for the meanings of Japanese terms used throughout this chapter.

All that is really necessary is the patience and care to produce a good product. The steps below represent an outline for producing a classic, undecorated saya for an inexpensive blade. They can easily be adapted to accommodate any sized blade of classical Japanese design. Pockets for accessories (*kazuka, kogai*), carvings or other custom features can all be added to this basic design. Figured wood may be substituted and a clear finish can be used to display the grain. Only imagination and a sense of taste limit the possibilities. It is well to keep in mind however that understatement is the hallmark of Zen influenced art.

Materials and Tools

The author's favorite domestic wood for saya is poplar. It is inexpensive, light, works cleanly, resists splitting and is easy to find. It is somewhat harder to carve than the Japanese Magnolia (*ho*) that is used for a traditional saya. The Magnolia actually works more like the basswood found in the U.S., which is a reasonable substitute for poplar, but harder to find and usually more expensive. Never use resinous wood such as pine, fir or cedar as it will eventually damage the blade.

It is convenient to work with half-inch true stock. If that cannot be purchased, thicker stock can be sawn or planed to the correct thickness. Look for pieces with a straight or gently curved, even grain, usually quarter sawn, with no knots or twists. Just like Magnolia, poplar is often a mixture of green and white wood. The color doesn't make any difference if an opaque finish is planed; otherwise white wood is desirable.

The *kurigata* (eye for attaching a belt-cord) and the caps for the *koiguchi* and *kojiri* (ends of the saya) can be made from a variety of materials. The author routinely uses domestic hedge (Osage Orange), a yellow wood that is very hard and resists splitting. Most other dense hardwoods—such as rosewood, ebony or cocobolo—will serve just as well. A traditional split resistant material to use is water buffalo horn, which can be purchased from domestic suppliers. Other possibilities include cow horn, ivory, deer antler or a plastic such as mycarta.

All these materials can be formed using similar techniques. Another option is to cast them out of epoxy resin. The best tools to use are on ones you are familiar with. Table 1 is offered only to suggest some of the options available to get the job done.

TABLE I
- a sheet of construction paper or cardboard
- calipers and/or ruler
- hand rip-saw and crosscut saw or table saw

- jig-saw or coping saw
- band-saw (not critical but very useful)
- table belt-sander (not critical but very useful)
- carving knife – Japanese utility knife is perfect
- 1/4" and 1/2" straight chisels
- curved gouge about 3/8" wide
- block plane of either American or Japanese design
- sanding block and garnet paper, grit sizes 60, 150, 220
- flat bastard file, 1/8" chain-saw sharpening file
- vise and hand drill, or drill press, 3/16" drill bit small triangular file
- water-proof buffing paper, 320 grit, 600 grit
- sandable undercoat, either aerosol or brushable
- soft hair watercolor brush 3/8 to 1/2" wide
- opaque laqueur or enamel, aerosol or brushable
- appropriate glue depending on individual needs
- bottle of Heavy oil or STP® Oil Treatment (epoxy, hide glue, PVA carpenter's glue)

A Japanese saya smith probably spends as much time sharpening his tools as he does slicing wood. Only a sharp tool will make a clean cut with minimal effort. Trying to cut with dull tools not only leaves a rough surface, but the extra force needed is likely to result in an eventual accident. Likewise, when using tools in general remember that when you get tired, you get dangerous—to your work and to yourself.

Layout

The basic shape of the saya is determined by the curve of the blade. A pattern can be made by tracing this curve off the blade onto a sheet of firm paper. Then trace a similar curve parallel to the first. Carry the lines out 1-2" past the length of the blade, depending on how much saya you want between the saya's closed end (*kojiri*) and the blade tip. The distance between the two lines should be twice the amount of wood you want covering the back of the blade and its edge plus the height of the blade at its widest part. Don't forget to allow enough wood at the saya's open end (*koiguchi*) to allow for the extra thickness of the metal sleeve (*habaki*) that fits between the tang and the blade. It is easiest to make these lines parallel to begin with even if you intend for the saya to taper eventually. As construction continues, the thickness of the saya's open end cap will pull the blade back out from the inside of the saya about 3/16" as it has just been marked out, but that's fine for now. The other thing to be kept in mind is that each end of the saya will need to be cut perpendicular to the tangent of the curve at that point, something that is tricky to "eyeball." This will often result in about an 1/8" of eventual shortening of the saya blank. It is not a bad plan to allow a little extra in all these initial measurements as sometimes more wood gets removed than expected or a cut must be made twice to get the direction correct. As a final step, trace the blade in the center of the paper saya, just to get a feeling for how much wood surrounds the blade. This represents your absolute margin for error and a double check that you have a pattern that leaves enough surrounding wood. Figure 1 shows what such a pattern might look like.

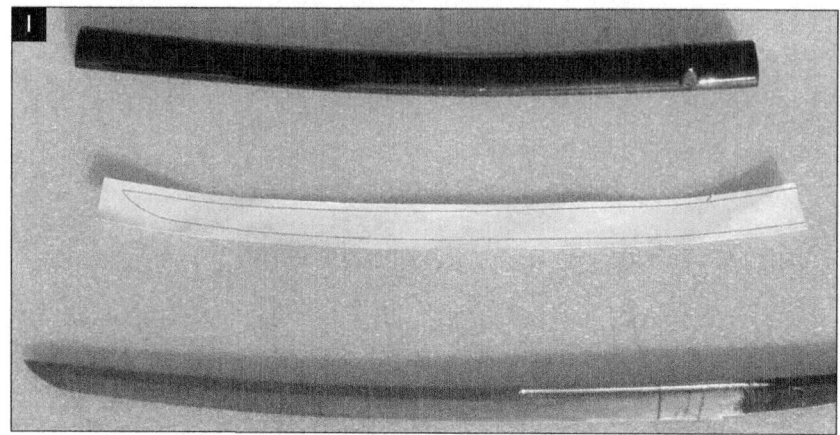

Figure 1: Paper pattern in center flanked by the wakizashi blade and finished saya.

Transfer the pattern onto the surface of the wood you are using. In the process you want as much of the board's grain to run parallel to the saya as possible.

A board with a gradual curve to the grain that matches the curve of the saya is ideal. More often, however, the grain will be straight. Since the open end of the saya is much more likely to be split, and requires substantially more carving than the closed end, line the grain up with the open end of the saya and allow the grain to cross diagonally across the distal end (Figure 2).

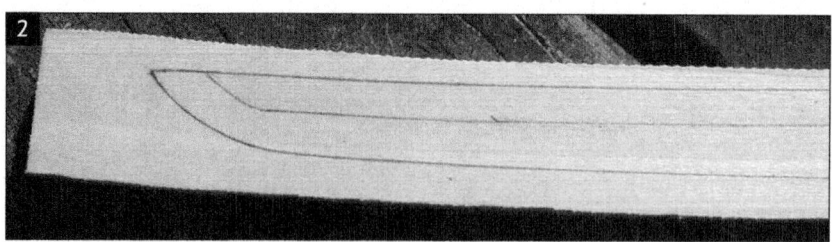

Figure 2: The grain of the wood runs slightly diagonally across the tip of this soon-to-be saya.

Cutting Out the Blanks

After the two blanks have been marked off on the board, they are cut out. This is most easily accomplished using a band saw. Using a wide (e.g. 1/2") blade will limit the number and degree of irregularities in the curve that you cut. A hand coping saw can also be used. Alternatively, the blanks may be cut out inside the straight lines of a rectangle using a hand or a table saw, and then the curved surfaces made using a plane or chisel (Figure 3). If using the later method, remember that all plane or chisel cuts must be made in the direction of the grain (Figure 4). If cutting results in the tearing of the wood surface, turn the work around and cut from the opposite direction. Don't forget, the grain often changes direction along a piece of wood, especially one that is curved in shape.

Figure 3: The saya blank is enclosed within a rectangle. The end is being cut off square with the crosscut side of a Japanese cabinet-maker's saw. The extra (hatched) wood will be removed next with a plane or chisel.

Figure 4: Plane cutting in the direction with the grain will take off clean shavings. Reversing the direction of the plane will tear up the grain and/or split the wood.

Inletting the Blanks

Once the blanks approximate each other in shape, the outline of the blade is inletted into each inner surface. Be sure to clearly mark the inside/outside, as well as the *koiguchi/kojiri* (saya's ends) relationships of each blank relative to the other before beginning. All blades are not symmetric and carving the inlet into the wrong surface or in the wrong direction may result in a mismatch when the blanks are glued together.

Make sure that the open end of the blank has been cut perpendicular. Mark the blade with a magic-marker or pencil where the metal sleeve (*habaki*) ends on the tang and then remove the sleeve, placing it in a safe place. Lay the blade on the blank with the mark you just made right at the edge of the open end of the blank. Center the blade on the blank, keeping the back of the blade parallel to the convex edge of the blank. Then trace the shape of the blade onto the blank (Figure 5a).

If you're using a regular lead pencil and holding it perfectly vertical while tracing, notice that your outline will be slightly too large. Finally, using the back of the blade, draw in the approximate location of the blade's side ridge. After this step, you will have three lines converging on the blade's tip (*mune*, *shinogi*, and *ha* lines) as it appears in Figure 2.

Figure 5a: The blanks have been cut out on a band saw and the blade place on top of one to check its size and, if correct, to trace the silhouette of the blade onto the blank.

Using a "V" gouge, bead the three lines mentioned above, being mindful of the tendency of the grain to pull the gouge off the line. The line representing the sword's back and side ridges should be roughly as deep as half the thickness of the blade. The line representing the sword's sharp edge should be more shallow (Figures 5b, c). The beads are then joined by chiseling out the intervening wood with 1/4" and 1/2" chisels and the curved gouge (Figures 6a, b).

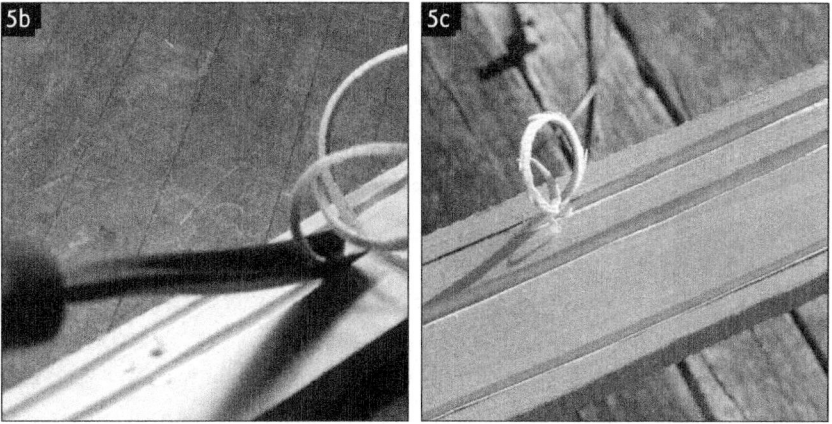

Figure 5b-c: The gouge has made deeper cuts for the mune and shinogi, and a more shallow ha.

Figure 6a-b: The beads made with the gouge have been joined at their depth with a straight chisel and curved gouge to receive one-half the blade.

When the shape of the blade has been inletted, the size and depth can be checked by sliding the blade in and out of the half of the saya you have created. To protect the blade during these maneuvers, the author has found it useful to coat the blade with STP® Oil Treatment which will prevent finger marks, scratches and moisture from harming the blade. It also serves another purpose. When the inletting is approaching the half-silhouette of the blade, you will be able to identify the remaining high points in your carving by their shiny, oily tops. By sliding the oily blade in and out of the saya and planing off the oil left on the wood you will eventually get a good close fit. Soot or lipstick also work well for this purpose but are harder to clean up afterwards.

After one blank has been inletted to your satisfaction, transfer the measurements of your carving to the other blank. Using calipers can facilitate this. Otherwise use a ruler to transfer the line for sword's curve from one blank to the other, and then use the blade for a tracing as before.

Originally, saya were glued together using an aged rice paste. This could be easily cracked open, which allowed the inside of a saya to be cleaned from time to time and then glued back together again. In order to keep the sword's edge from opening this joint during carrying and drawing, one side of the saya was inletted deeper than exactly half the blade thickness, and the other slightly less than half. This kept the sword's edge from riding on the glue joint when the two halves were assembled. The use of modern glues often makes this process unnecessary. Another feature of some classic saya is a small hollowed out reservoir beyond the sword tip to collect blood from the replaced blade.

After inletting both blanks, they should be assembled with cord, or "C" clamps and the blade past in and out its new saya. Tight spots are identified by the oil and planed off (Figure 7). This is tiresome, but the only way to get a good fit. The blade should not rub at any point except along its back. Don't keep taking off high spots to excess, however, or the blade will rattle in the saya. Once the blade fits well, the sleeve (*habaki*) should be replaced on the tang and space for it carved into the end of each side of the saya to accommodate it (Figure 8). This must fit tightly and you must also allow for the thickness of the cap that will be placed on this end (usually 3/16" to 1/4"). Finally, if the saya is for a practice blade, the inletting may be lightly sanded. Since this might leave grit that could scratch a finely polished blade, sanding should be avoided for valuable blades.

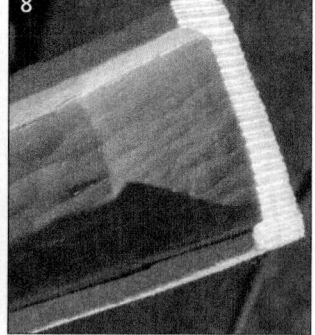

Figure 7: Two halves have been joined without glue and the oily blade is being slid in and out of the inlet to identify high spots. Note the oak block used under the clamp.

Figure 8: The saya's open end has been carved out to accept the habaki.

Jointing the Two Halves of the Saya

The two halves of the saya are simply glued together and clamped until the glue of choice has cured or dried. But there are some problems to consider. First, what glue should you use? If you are making a saya for a practice blade, the choice may simply be what's available. The author started out using Carpenter's glue of either the white or yellow persuasion. It cured in about two hours and was quite strong. When a saya was made for a live blade however, it was found that over time, the glue appeared to discolor the steel.

If the saya is to be opened for cleaning, hide glue—which is prepared by mixing it with and equal volume of water and heating it—works very well. It is strong and brittle, allowing the two halves of the saya to be split apart without damaging the wood. The tops of violins are actually glued on in this way, and are 'popped off' for prolonged storage of the instrument.

More recently, the author has come to use epoxy glues. These are very strong (essentially fiberglass) and, unlike other glues, can fill significant gaps in the joints, or other holes or defects in the work. They are stronger than the wood so the sword's edge can rest upon a joint that is very solid and non-reactive.

Using an epoxy with a half hour set time allows some adjustment when gluing the sides together. These completely cure in about twelve hours. For gluing on the eyepiece holding the belt-cord (*kurigata*) and caps, or for making minor repairs or fills, epoxy that sets up in five minutes works well and is good to go in a couple of hours. With either type, you must be careful to mix equal amounts of glue and resin or it will never set up!

Another consideration in the process of creating the glue joint is the bead of glue that gets squeezed out of the joint and into the inside of the saya. This has the potential of keeping the blade from fitting all the way into the saya and depending on the glue, could damage a good blade. To some extent you control this by using the least amount of glue necessary for the job. Apply it to both sides before joining them. Some glue however is still going to run. This is where the STP comes in again. The two saya halves are joined and clamped, but before the glue can set, the blade (with the sleeve, *habaki*) coated with STP can be slid in and out of the saya once, pushing the glue out of the way. The blade should then be immediately wiped clean with a cloth—and a solvent, if necessary, depending on the glue used. This is probably not appropriate for a live blade, at least an expensive one. In this case, the saya maker is probably well advised to have make a wooden model of the blade ahead of time to use for this purpose.

Clamping the two halves of the saya together should be done in the proper manner. Clamps should not be applied directly to the work. They leave crush marks that damage the surface. Furthermore, if you place a clamp in the middle of an inletted side there is the risk of splitting the work, or at least creating a permanent convexity on the inside wall which will interfere with the fit. To prevent both of these problems, blocks as wide as the saya halves are slipped between the clamps and the saya. This puts the main pressure on the edges, not the center of each half (see Figure 7). Wooden furniture clamps eliminate the need to do this. The original method of holding the sides together as the glue dried was to wrap a cord up and down the two halves. This required holding the saya in each hand and the cord in your mouth, so strong solid teeth were essential to the classical saya maker. The cord tends to crush the outside edges of the two blanks, although they are the next things to be removed.

There is an alternative method of getting to this point in saya construction that, while not suitable for a live blade, works well for a practice blade and requires less skill and minimal carving. Instead of making the saya from two inletted halves, think of making a sandwich with the two outer blanks flanking a third, thinner, inner layer. This central layer is shaped the same as the other two and then thinned to the thickness of the blade. Using either a band saw or a coping saw, the silhouette of the blade is cut from its center (Figure 9). It is then glued to one of the sidepieces. When dry, any glue run is removed from the inside and size adjustments are made to the cutout silhouette with a knife and/or chisel and the open end widened for the sleeve. The second side is then glued on.

Figure 9: As an alternative method, a central layer of wood the thickness of the blade as the silhouette of the blade cut out and then is sandwiched between two outer blanks, which require inletting for the habaki only.

This later technique results in a saya with a rectangular central hole, not one shaped like the cross section of the blade. Therefore there is no taper to cushion the sword's edge nor "V" to receive the top of the sword's back. It is, however, perfectly adequate as a saya for an inexpensive working blade, especially if made of very soft wood. If this method is adopted, remember that the tip of many blades widen slightly at the level of the *yakote*, which separates the tip from the blade: be sure to allow enough width to the center layer to accommodate this.

Shaping the Saya

Prior to this point, it was not necessary for the two halves to be identical. Now that they are joined, they must be made to appear to be a single piece of wood. In the process, the saya must be made symmetric and the curves "faired up." Any tapering of the saya must be performed and the cross section must be rounded symmetrically. "Fairing" refers to the removal of any bumps or irregularities along a curved surface. Unlike dealing with straight lines, curves are not easily measured and must be judged and corrected primarily by using the eye. One helpful guide is the use of a uniform shaped batten sprung along the curve to help identify high areas (Figure 10a, b).

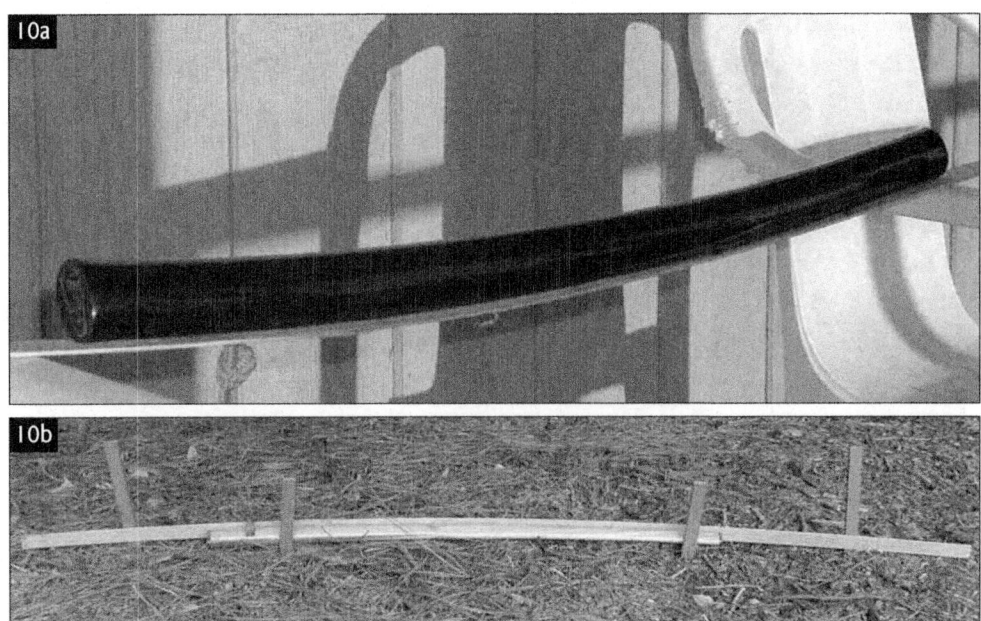

Figure 10a-b: Two ways of springing a batten to check the "fairness" of the curved edge of a saya.

Using a plane, the upper convex surface is carefully planed at right angles to the sides. The shape of the curve is frequently checked by holding the saya at eye level and sighting along the edge of the curve. Looking at the curve going away from you will accentuate irregularities you wouldn't see otherwise and is the second trick for insuring "fairness." The high spots are then planed off, which smoothes (fairs) the curve. The concave lower surface is then cleaned up in a similar fashion. During this planing, careful attention will have to be focused on the direction of the grain. When planing the convex surface of the saya, for example, it is often necessary to cut from both ends towards the center. Since grain is in three dimensions, one side may need to be planed in an entirely different direction that the other side, depending on how you originally laid out the blanks. When this task is completed, the cross-section of the saya should be the same rectangle at all points along its length.

Once the saya is a uniform rectangle from one end to the other, the tapering can be done. While still keeping the cross-section a rectangle, use a plane to taper the saya from the open end to the closed end. Generally the height will be reduced by only a 1/16" or so, and the width by a 1/2" or less depending on the blade's length. This small amount of taper gives the saya a pleasant appearance without being obvious. It is very easy to overdo this tapering. Care must also be taken to taper in a uniform fashion, especially the sides which must maintain a flat, not curved surface. Avoid sharpening the closed end like a pencil. A belt sander is useful to cut the side taper since the surface remains flat, but it can quickly remove too much wood if used aggressively.

After establishing the proper taper, the saya is rounded using a plane. The following technique is recommend as allowing visual clues to keeping the rounding symmetric from side to side, and uniform and fair, the entire length of one side. First plane each corner off turning the cross-sectional rectangle into an octagon. Use as a guide the width of the new surface of the octagon being created, remembering that it must taper uniformly toward the closed end. Also notice the distance of the newly created corner from the midline glue joint of the top of the saya and the distance towards the center of the face. The octagon can then be inspected and evened up by eye.

Next, do the same thing one more time, taking off each of the eight corners by turning them into uniform, fair, tapering planes. Once again, even it all up by inspecting and modifying the planes. Only then, when all the newly formed shallow corners appear to be tapering evenly towards the closed end should shallow plane cuts be used to knock off these corners and turn the cross-section into a near ellipse. Take care of the tendency to remove too much from the koiguchi and kojiri, and too little from the area 2-3" back from the open end. This is more likely to occur using a western "push plane" as opposed to the use of a traditional Japanese "draw plane" (Figure 3). This is also the stage when, in an effort to correct irregularities, the width of the remaining wood can be misjudged and the center cavity entered, usually on the convex edge of the saya. (If that happens don't give up in despair, the hole can probably be filled with epoxy and never show under a paint job). Finally the saya is sanded parallel to the grain using #60 grit emery paper wrapped around a wooden block. Traditional woodworkers in Japan do not use sandpaper, but smooth their work with progressively shallower plane cuts and finish with a very mild silicon abrasive made of plant stems. Remember that even sandpaper can take off too much wood rather quickly. These steps are illustrated in Figures 11a-d.

Figure 11a-b-c-d: The saya undergoes a systematic transformation from square to oval and finally sanded smooth with coarse garnet paper.

Adding End Caps

Before completely shaping the saya, the end caps for the koiguchi and kojiri should be fashioned and attached. Any hardwood, bone, antler or plastic cut into a sheet may be used. If a hardwood is utilized, make sure the grain follows the long axis of the ellipse. Place the closed end of the saya on the sheet of material close to one end and trace that end onto the sheet with a pencil. This will result in a slightly larger cap than the saya needs, but that is what you want initially. Then cut the cap out, making sure it will completely cover the end of the saya. Glue it to the kojiri, making sure it overlaps the sides of the saya all the way around.

Fashioning the cap for the open end requires a little more finesse. At an inch or so away from the edge of the sheet of cap material, mark the cross-sectional shape of your sleeve (*habaki*). To do this use a template cut from a piece of cardboard or an index card (Figure 12). Drill several holes inside the template for the sleeve and cut out the inside of this area with either a jigsaw or a coping saw (Figure 13a, b). Then enlarge the hole with an appropriately shaped file, remembering to slope the sides of the hole to match the taper of the sleeve.

Frequent matching to the sleeve will prevent removing too much material, which would allow the sleeve to fall right through. It is generally wise to fit the cap so that there is about 1/8" of the sleeve left sticking out from the cap when placed within it. This will quickly wear in deeper with a working saya. Place the sleeve into the cap, and then place both into the saya. Then trace the saya end onto the cap blank and cut it out with a saw, keeping it if anything a little larger than necessary.

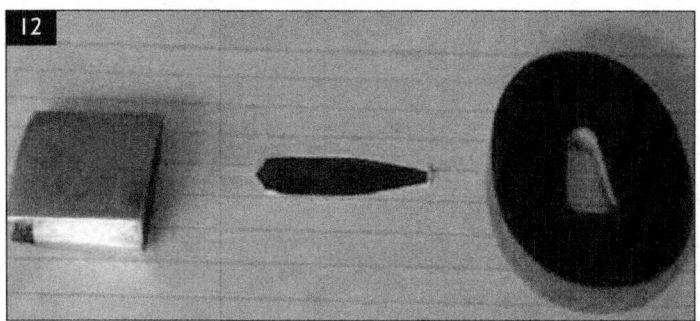

Figure 12: A template made from the widest part of the habaki (left) and a commercial buffalo horn blank (right) to be fashioned into the cap for the koiguchi.

Figure 13a-b: On the left, several holes have been drilled to facilitate cutting out the pattern as shown on the right.

Gluing the cap on requires very careful placement, since if it is off-center at all, the blade will bind when the sword is sheathed. Using the blade and the sleeve as guides during the gluing process can prevent this. Again, coat the sleeve and the blade with STP. Put the fitted cap on the sleeve loosely and then put the minimum of glue necessary on the top of the open end of the saya. Place the sword and sleeve into the saya loosely, staying away as much as possible from any glue (Figure 14). Squeeze the cap onto the surface of the saya, hold the cap firmly against the saya, and remove the blade and sleeve. If the cap slips, add some glue and try the maneuver again. Place the saya upright to dry. Immediately clean the blade and sleeve of any glue. Quick drying (about five minute) epoxy works very well for this, although watersoluble glue such as hide or carpenter's glue would be safer for a valuable blade.

Figure 14:
Gluing an oversized cap of hedge on to the unfinished saya using the sleeve and blade as position guides. This cap will have to be inletted for a utility blade. Also notice the sleeve does not go all the way into the cap to allow for later fitting and wear.

Once the glue holding the caps has dried, the caps can be filed or sanded to remove the overlap and make them flush with the outer surface of the saya. Avoid the tendency to angle the cap edge away from the saya in an attempt to protect the saya from harm. Tape can be used to protect the saya from scratches or gouges during this process (Figure 15). After the sides are parallel to the saya, the face of the caps may be shaped, for example the closed end may be slightly rounded or the open end inletted slightly (Figure 16). Once the caps are shaped to your satisfaction, the entire saya including caps should be sanded in the direction of the grain with a series of 100, 150 and 225 grit paper.

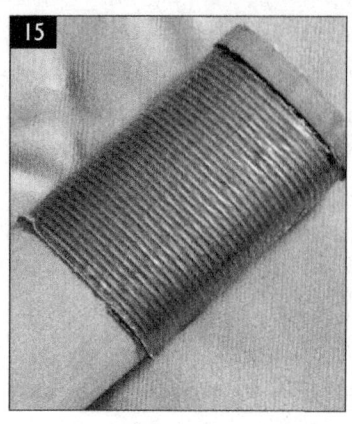

Figure 15: This open end cap of hedge is about to be filed even with the sides of the saya body, which is being protected from file damage by a piece of duct tape.

Figure 16: A finished end cap of deer antler sanded flush with the sides of the saya. Its corners have been rounded with a file and garnet paper.

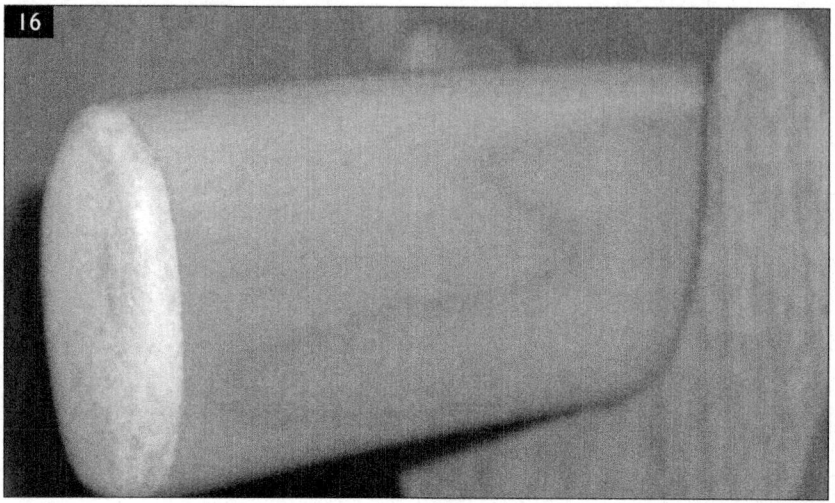

Making and Fitting the Kurigata

As with the caps, the belt cord fitting (*kurigata*) can be made of any hardwood, bone, horn or plastic available. The process is essentially the same for any material and consists mostly of grinding in one guise or another. Figure 17 illustrates the sequential steps in forming a kurigata, in this case, out of birch. A block of the appropriate thickness is formed into a trapezoid with a saw. The base is then recessed with a file, saw or sanding wheel. Three (or more) holes are drilled through the block at the middle and the extremes of the hole through which the belt cord will pass. The sides of the trapezoid are then tapered with either a sander or a file so it is more like a pyramid. The top is then rounded and reduced in thickness. Round files used for sharpening chain saws are used to join and enlarge the central hole. Finally, files and sandpaper are used to round and smooth the entire block. Many variations of shape were used in the past, but most were kept simple and symmetric.

Figure 17: From 12 o'clock clockwise, a block is progressively fashioned into a kurigata as described in the text. The finished kurigata is in the center.

Once fashioned, the kurigata must be attached to the saya. This must be after the fine sanding but before any sealer or finish is applied. The base of the kurigata may be filed to approximate the curve of the saya and glued right to its surface. Alternatively and more attractive, a groove may be cut or filed into the outerside of the saya to receive the kurigata (Figure 18a, b). The author prefers a combination of the above. After the kurigata is glued in place, the saya is ready to be finished.

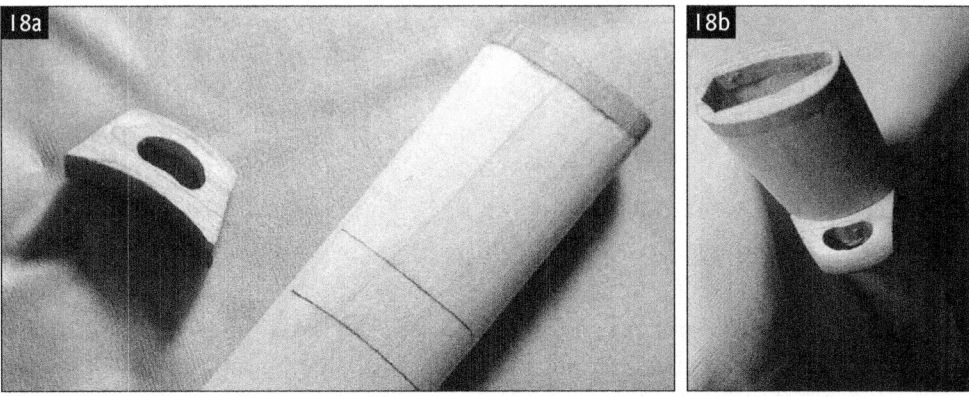

Figure 18a-b: A groove is cut or filed into the saya between the lines and the kurigata inserted into it and glued. This saya has a birch kurigata and hedge caps.

Finishing the Saya

However the saya is to be finished, the end result should be a smooth finish without any grain or other variations of the wood showing thorough. The most forgiving finish for a beginner is probably a clear one because the grain pattern of the wood disguises any imperfections in the finish. Several of the rub-on finishes of oil and varnish made for gunstocks work very nicely on a saya. If this option is elected, however, your glue joints and matching of caps and kurigata to the saya will be quite visible.

An opaque finish is far more traditional, the usual being a shinny black lacquer. There is nothing less forgiving however, than a shinny black finish. Just like on a black Porsche, every scratch and irregularity shows! Dull and textured finishes may prove to be a good compromise for the amateur saya maker as they cover poor fitting and don't emphasize surface blemishes. Also remember that some saya were wrapped with leather, cane, cord or ray skin—any of which eliminates much of the worry about the final finish.

The basis of any finish is the filling of the wood pores and other irregularities with a thick layer of undercoat. For a transparent finish, this can be done with water-soluble wood filler-sealer, or many coats of clear lacquer, enamel, or acrylic finish. Before the first coat of under coat or filler is applied, the saya should be wet with water and allowed to dry, this will raise any splinters and feathery grain. After drying, it should be lightly sanded with 225 grit paper, and then the undercoat applied. It is generally better to put many light coats of finish on over a period of time than to try to do it all with a couple of thick coats. This can be accomplished with a brush, aerosol cans or an airbrush. Sanding in between each coat with 320 grit finishing paper will result in better fill and a uniform surface. When the sanded saya shows no apparent irregularities, the external coat should be begun.

Japanese lacquer (*urushi*) is very expensive and hard to work with. It is quite toxic as it contains the active ingredient of Poison Oak. A synthetic Japanese product, under the trade name "Cashew," is available in this country and has many of the attributes of urushi without the toxicity. It should be thinned with turpentine. If lacquer thinner is used, there is a good chance the topcoat will cause a crackling of the previous coat thus requiring its removal. Both of these products are difficult to apply smoothly and dry very slowly. On the other hand, the quality of the surface in terms of depth and gloss is worth the work of learning to use them if your woodworking skill deserves the best finish. Good quality American lacquer can be purchased from woodworking supply stores. Use a soft fur watercolor brush to apply it and be sure to thin it sufficiently prior to application. Special brushing lacquer thinner can be found as well. Aerosol lacquer from the hardware store varies greatly in make-up and quality. If lacquer is chosen, be prepared to use 10-15 coats with wet sanding with 600 grit wet/dry sandpaper just like you'd refinish an automobile. When using lacquer, remember that one coat softens the previous one. So, if you wipe off a drip or run it will result in a crater that will have to be filled. It is better to let any drips dry thoroughly and then sand them down.

Aerosol cans of enamel intended to touch-up farm implements (John Deere Green, Ford Blue, etc.) provide hard, durable coverage while being fairly forgiving. With any aerosol or sprayer, don't get too close to the work and don't apply enough to cause a run—the curse of the spray can. If each side is alternately sprayed repeatedly, an eventual overlap on the top and the bottom of the saya will appear. Each coat should be lightly sanded before the application of the next. It is better to vary the direction from which the spray occurs or rotate the saya during the spraying process. A thin strip of cedar shingle is perfect for supporting the saya during spraying (Figures 19a, b). Also, don't forget that the spray goes all over the place, so don't spray in a close space or near anything you don't want discolored. Avoid wind and dust.

As a final encouragement to be creative, remember that whatever you initially spread on your saya, if you don't like it you can sand it off, call the residual "filler" and refinish it with something else.

Figure 19a-b: Saya supported by a 1-inch strip of shingle undergoing finishing with an aerosol lacquer.

GLOSSARY

ha	the sharp edge of the sword blade
habaki	the sleeve between tang and blade that wedges the blade into the saya
iaito	non-ferrous practice sword
kashu	type of synthetic Japanese lacquer
kazuka	utility blade carried in a pocket in some saya
kissaki	the tip of the blade
kogai	a skewer-like tool and ear cleaner stored in some saya
koiguchi	the open end of the saya into which the sword is placed
kojiri	the tip of the closed end of the saya
kurigata	the fitting through which the belt cord is attached to the saya
maharba	the widest part of the blade, usually just in front of the habaki
mune	the top of the back of the blade, usually "V" shaped
nakago	the tang
sageo	the cord attaching the saya to the belt (*obi*)
same	ray-skin leather used to wrap the sword handle
saya ate	two saya colliding out of carelessness of the wearer(s)
shinogi	the side ridge of a blade
sori	the amount of curvature of a blade from habaki to kissaki
urushi	true Japanese lacquer—the sap of the urushi tree
wakizashi	shorter companion sword of a two sword set (daisho)
yakote	a vertical ridge separating the tip from the blade

References

Kapp, L., Kapp, H., & Yoshihara, Y. (1987). *The craft of the Japanese sword*. Tokyo: Kodansha International Ltd.

Young, W. (1998). *The glue book*. Newtown, CT: The Taunton Press.

Sword-Cutting Practice of Feudal Japan: Anatomical Considerations of Tameshigiri

by Peter J. Ward, Ph.D.

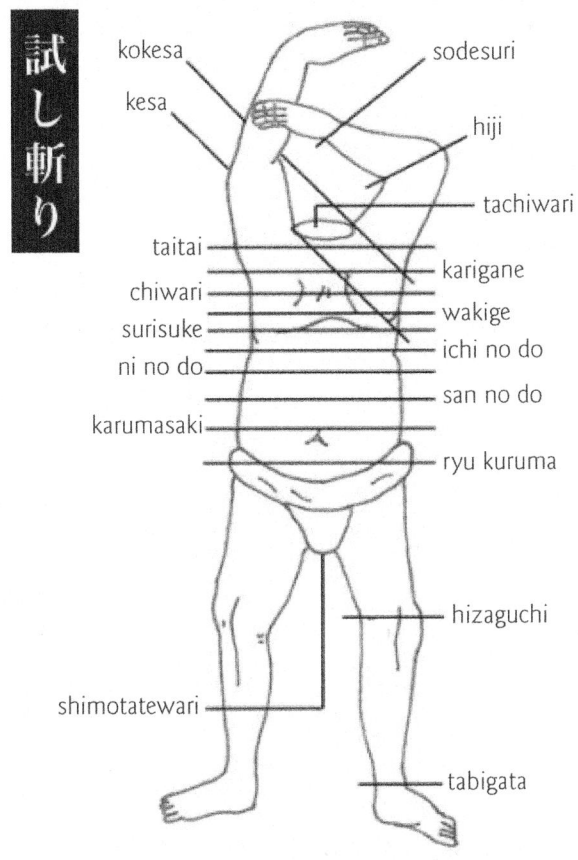

Figure 1: This diagram demonstrates the placement of each cut on the body during tameshigiri.

Introduction

Tameshigiri, or test cutting, was extensively practiced in feudal Japan. While stationary objects were often used in this practice, it was common to use the bodies of executed criminals to test the cutting abilities of swords and the swordsmen themselves. In this practice, the body was taken to an area containing a mount of sand that was built with bamboo poles projecting upward. The sand mound and poles were used to position the body so a powerful stroke could be delivered to specific targets.

Tameshigiri was relatively common during the era preceding the Warring States period (starting in the sixteenth century) of Japan and is documented as having been extensively practiced by members of the samurai class during the seventeenth century. At that time, Japan was united under a single military leader, the shogun Tokugawa Ieyasu. Under the Tokugawa shogunate there were fewer armed conflicts within Japan, and tameshigiri was used as a way to maintain the "warrior spirit" of the samurai. The practice remained widespread within the samurai class into the eighteenth century. During the eighteenth century, as the samurai class transitioned from full-time warriors to bureaucrats, the grotesque aspects of tameshigiri clashed with the more elegant persona of the samurai civil servant.

Tameshigiri was used primarily to grade the quality of blades that were produced by swordsmiths. Despite no longer being at war, the paired swords (one long *katana* and one shorter *wakizashi*) remained the symbol of the samurai class, and their quality was of great concern. During this time, tameshigiri was left to a select group of lower-status samurai who were professional blade testers. This role often remained within specific family lineages, such as the Yamada family. The practice continued into the nineteenth century, until the whole social strata of Japan was reordered by the Meiji Restoration in 1868. The practice of tameshigiri on the bodies of executed criminals ceased at this time (Joy & Hogitaro, 1963; Kremer, 2008; Takeuchi, 2009).

Objectives of This Study

The historical records related to tameshigiri primarily list the early high status samurai who conducted the practice, the professional sword testers who inherited it, and the executed criminals upon whose bodies the cuts were delivered. Little information has been presented on the cuts themselves. The purpose of this study is to use original diagrams that detail the cuts and correlate them with the anatomical structures that would have been encountered by a blade as it passed through the body. This study will list the structures involved in each tameshigiri cut and conjecture on the factors that contributed to the difficulty of each cut.

Methods

The name, placement, and difficulty of each cut were taken from the seminal work on this topic in English (Joly & Hogitaro, 1963) and are shown in figure 1 (See first page of this chapter). The Yamada family, a lineage of professional *suemonoshi* (test cutters), listed the difficulty of each cut. In order of increasing difficulty, the cuts are as follows:

1) sodesuri (figure 2)
2) tabigata (figure 3)
3) kokesa (figure 4)
4) ichi no do (figure 5)
5) ni no do (figure 6)
6) san no do (figure 7)
7) shimotateware (not pictured)
8) suritsuke (figure 8)
9) kurumasaki (figure 9)
10) wakige (figure 10)
11) tachiwari (figure 11)
12) kesa (figure 12)
13) chiwari (figure 13)
14) karigane (figure 14)
15) taitai (figure 15)
16) ryo kuruma (figure 16)

The Visible Human slice viewer (http://visiblehuman) was accessed to create a "slice" that replicated each of the cuts from the Joly and Hogitaro text. Once the images were harvested, the structures were identified and labeled.

Shimotatewari was not pictured. This exclusion was not our of squeamishness but because the extent of the cut was unclear. It might involve only the genitalia or might have been a sagittal cut of the pelvic bones. Given its placement in the list, the latter is more likely, but its exact dimensions are unknown. Two cuts present on the illustration (figure 1) were not listed, images of these two cuts, *hiji* (figure 17) and *hizaguchi* (figure 18), were gathered in the same way as the listed cuts.

Results

The thickest sections such as taitai (figure 15) and karigane (figure 14) all tended to be among the most difficult cuts. Not surprisingly, the smaller sections such as sodesuri (figure 2) and tabigata (figure 3) were the two least difficult cuts. However, it is also clear that the bony content of the cut is of prime importance. For example, the most difficult cut, ryu kuruma (figure 16), is very similar in size and sofe-tissue composition to kurumasaki (figure 9). However, ryu kuruma contains a significant amount of bone, while kurumasaki contains a single lumbar vertebra. Therefore, bony content is also determinant of the difficulty of each cut. This is in agreement with a forensic investigation of historical battleground remains showing that battlefield cuts were frequently deflected by bone (Karasulas, 2004).

Figure 1: This diagram demonstrates the placement of each cut on the body during tameshigiri. See the first page of this chapter for reference.

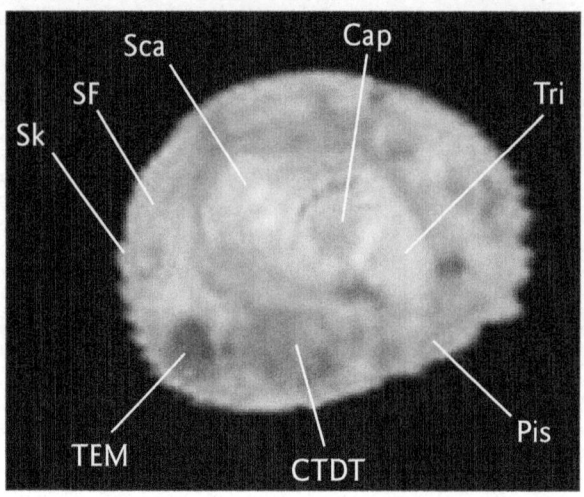

Figure 2: *Sodesuri* (wrist). Structures encountered —
    Cap: capitate   CTDT: carpal tunnel and digital flexor tendons
    Pis: pisiform   Sca: scaphoid
    SF: subcutaneous fat   Sk: skin
    TEM: thenar eminence muscles   Tri: triquetrum

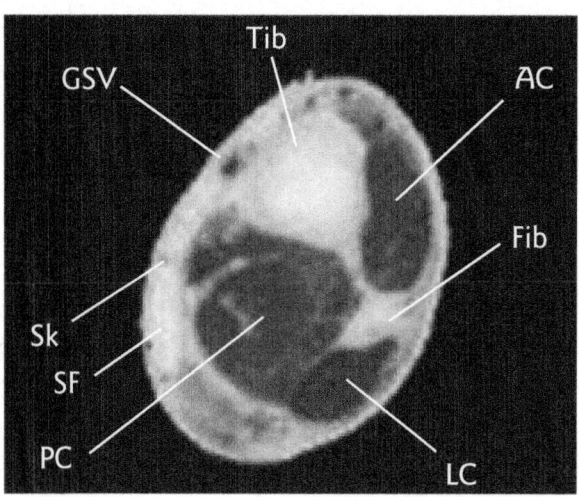

Figure 3: *Tabigata* (ankle).
Structures encountered —
    AC: anterior compartment of leg   Fib: fibula
    GSV: greater saphenous vein   LC: lateral compartment of leg
    PC: posterior compartment of leg   SF: subcutaneous fat
    Sk: skin   Tib: tibia

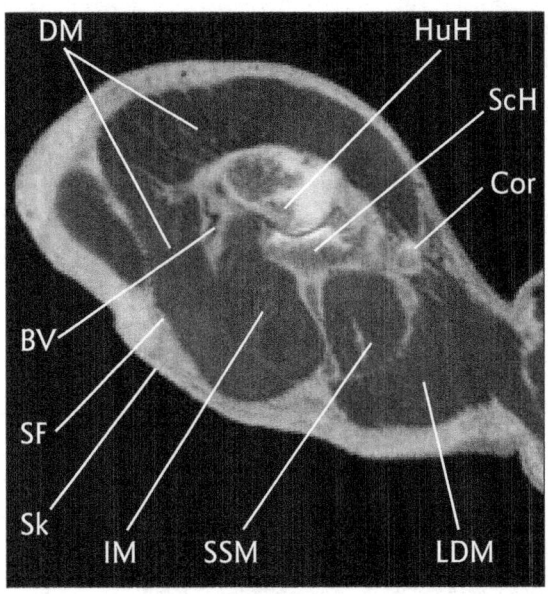

Figure 4: *Kokesa.*
Structures encountered —
- BV: brachial vessels
- Cor: coracoid process of scapula
- HuH: humeral head
- IM: infraspinatus muscle
- LDM: latissius dorsi muscle
- ScH: scapular head
- Sk: skin
- SSM: subscapularis muscle

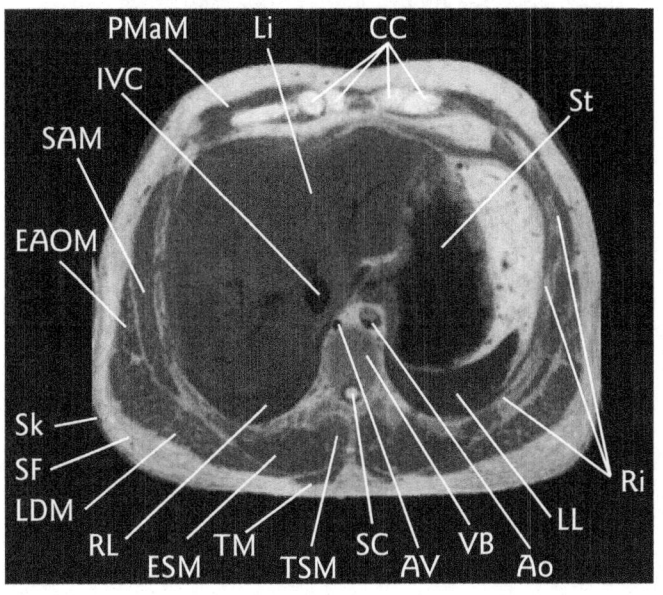

Figure 5: *Ichi no do.*
Structures encountered —
- Ao: aorta
- AV: azygos vein
- CC: costal cartilages
- EAOM: external abdominal oblique muscle
- ESM: erector spinae muscle
- IVC: inferior vena cava

LDM: latissimus dorsi muscle
LL: left lung
Ri: ribs
SAM: serratus anterior muscle
SF: subcutaneous fat
Sto: stomach
TSM: transversospinalis muscles

Li: liver
PMaM: pectoralis major muscle
RL: right lung
SC: spinal canal
Sk: skin
TM: trapezius muscle
VB: vertebral body

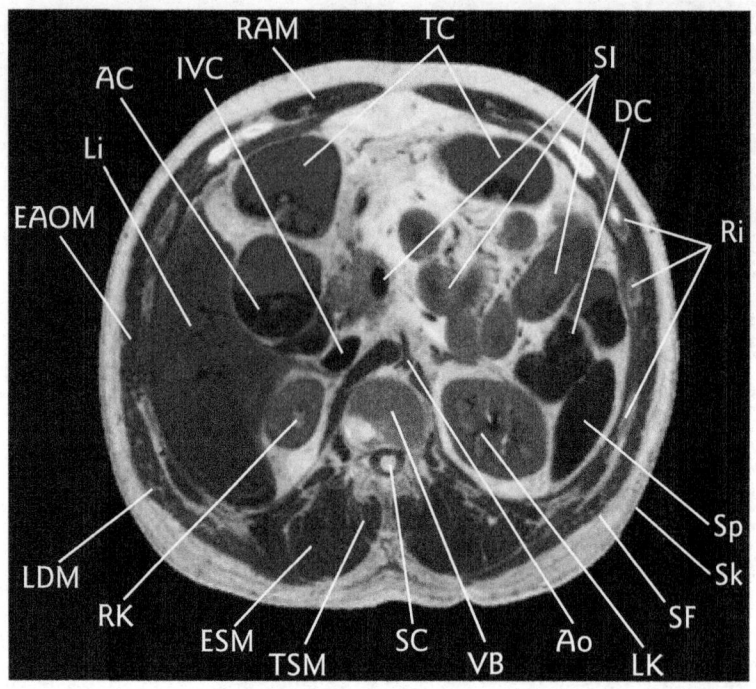

Figure 6: *Ni no do.* Structures encountered —

AC: ascending colon

Ao: aorta

DC: descending colon

EAOM: external abdominal oblique muscle

ESM: erector spinae muscle

IVC: inferior vena cava

LDM: latissimus dorsi muscle

Li: liver

LK: left kidney

RAM: rectus abdominis muscle

Ri: ribs

RK: right kidney

SC: spinal canal

SF: subcutaneous fat

SI: small intestines

Sk: skin

Sp: splean

TC: transverse colon

TSM: transversospinalis muscles

VB: vertebral body

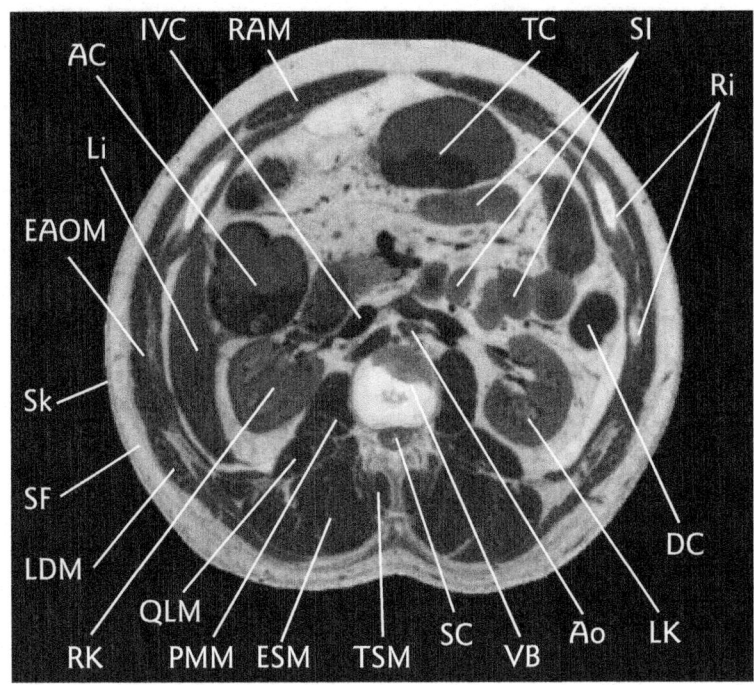

Figure 7: *San no do.* Structures encountered —

AC: ascending colon
DC: descending colon
ESM: erector spinae muscle
LDM: latissius dorsi muscle
LK: left kidney
PMM: psoa major muscle
Ri: ribs
SC: spinal canal
SI: small intestines
TC: transverse colon
VB: vertebral body (includes portion of internalvertebral disc)
Ao: aorta
EAOM: external abdominal oblique muscle
IVC: inferior vena cava
Li: liver
QLM: quadrattus lumborum muscle
RAM: rectus abdominis muscle
RK: right kidney
SF: subcutaneous fat
Sk: skin
TSM: transversospinalis muscles

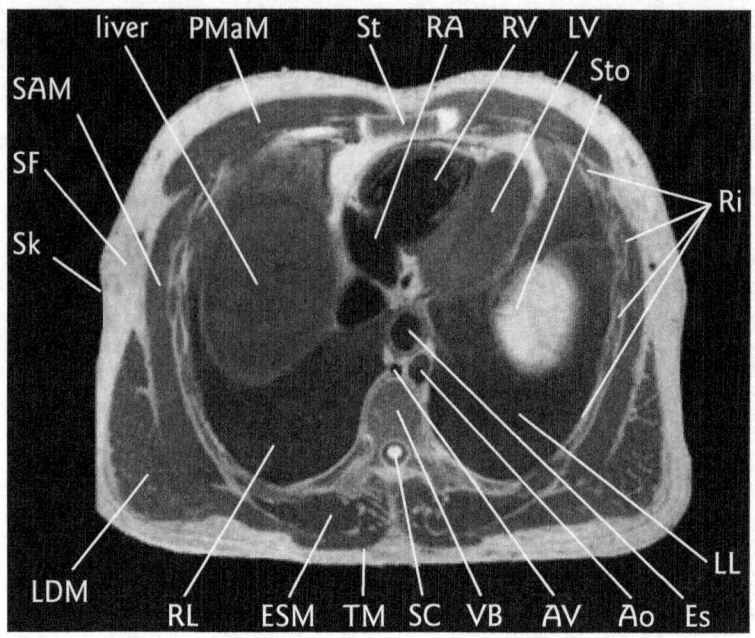

Figure 8: *Suritsuke*. Structures encountered —
Ao: aorta
AV: azygos vein
Es: esophagus
LDM: latissimus dorsi muscle
LL: left lung
LV: left ventricle
PMaM: pectoralis major muscle
RA: right atrium
Ri: ribs
RL: right lung
RV: right ventricle
SAM: serratus anterior muscle
SC: spinal canal
SF: subcutaneous fat
Sk: skin
St: sternum
Sto: stomach
TM: trapezius muscle
VB: vertebral body

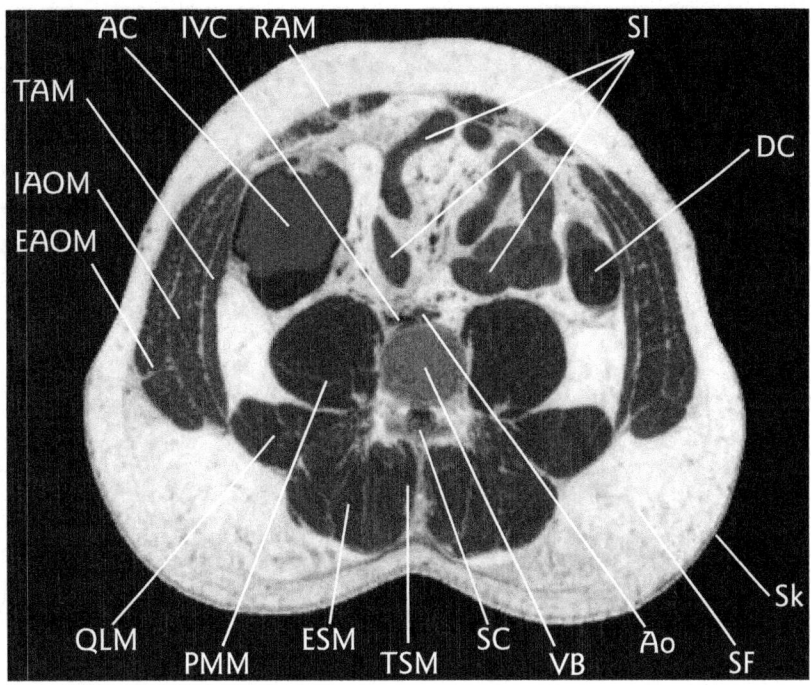

Figure 9: Structures encountered —
    AC: ascending colon
    Ao: aorta
    DC: descending colon
    EAOM: external abdominal oblique muscle
    ESM: erector spinae muscle
    IAOM: internal abdominal oblique muscle
    IVC: inferior vena cava
    QLM: quadrattus lumborum muscle
    PMM: psoas major muscle
    RAM: rectus abdominis muscle
    SC: spinal canal
    SF: subcutaneous fat
    SI: small intestines
    Sk: skin
    TAM: transversus abdominis muscle
    TSM: transversospinalis muscles
    VB: vertebral body

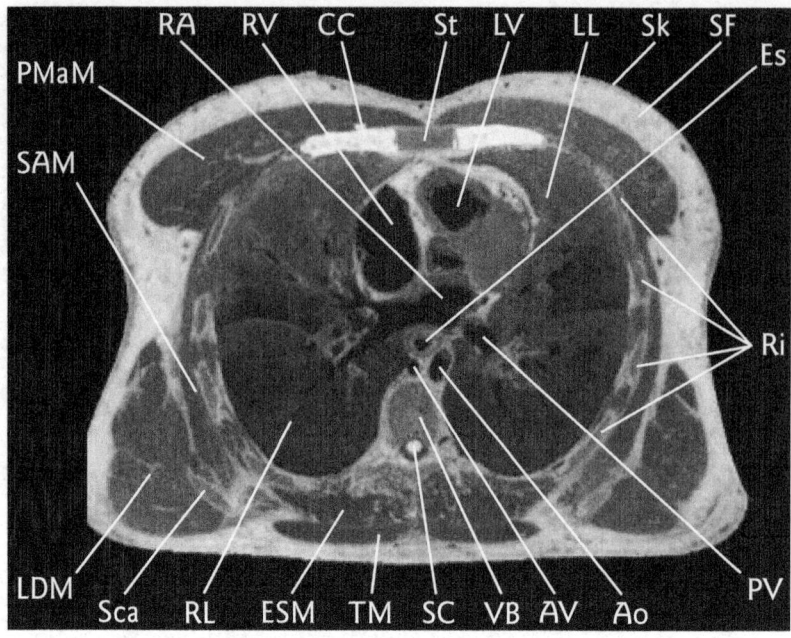

Figure 10: *Wakige*. Structures encountered —

Ao: aorta

AV: azygos vein

CC: costal cartilage

Es: esophagus

ESM: erector spinae muscles

LL: left ventricle

PMaM: pectoralis major muscle

PV: pulmonary vessels

RA: right atrium

Ri: ribs

RL: right lung

RV: right ventricle

SAM: serratus anterior muscle

SC: spinal canal

Sca: scapula

SF: subcutaneous fat

Sk: skin

St: sternum

TM: trapezius muscle

VB: vertebral body

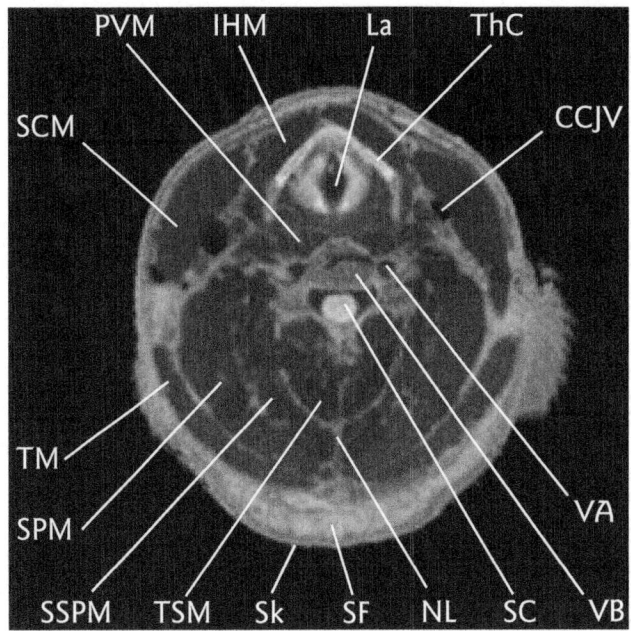

Figure 11: *Tachiwari*. Structures encountered —

CCJV: common carotid artery and jugular vein
IHM: infrahyoid muscles
La: larynx
NL: nuchal ligament
PVM: prevertebral muscles
SC: spinal canal
SCM: sternocleidomastoid muscle
SF: subcutaneous fat
Sk: skin
SPM: splenius muscles
SSPM: semispinalis muscles
SVC: superior vena cava
ThC: thyroid cartilage
TM: trapezius muscle
Tr: trachea
TSM: transversospinalis muscles
A: vertebral artery
VB: vertebral body

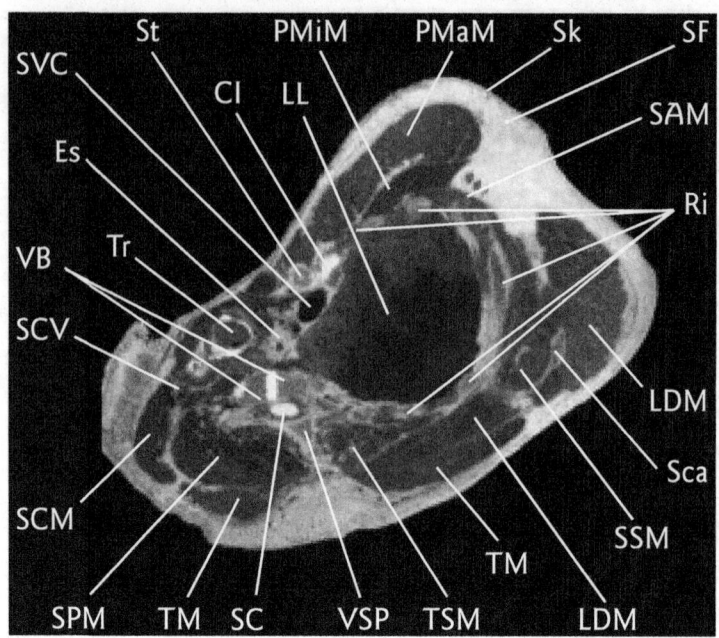

Figure 12: *Kesa*. Structures encountered —
  Cl: clavicle
  Es: esophagus
  LDM: latissimus dorsi muscle
  LL: left lung
  PMaM: pectoralis major muscle
  PMiM: pectoralis minor muscle
  Ri: ribs
  SAM: serratus anterior muscle
  SC: spinal canal
  Sca: scapula
  SCV: subclavian vessels
  SF: subcutaneous fat
  Sk: skin
  SPM: splenius muscles
  SSM: subscapularis muscle
  St: sternum
  SVC: superior vena cava
  TM: trapezius muscle
  TSM: transversospinalis muscles
  Tr: trachea
  VB: vertebral bodies
  VSP: vertebral spinous process

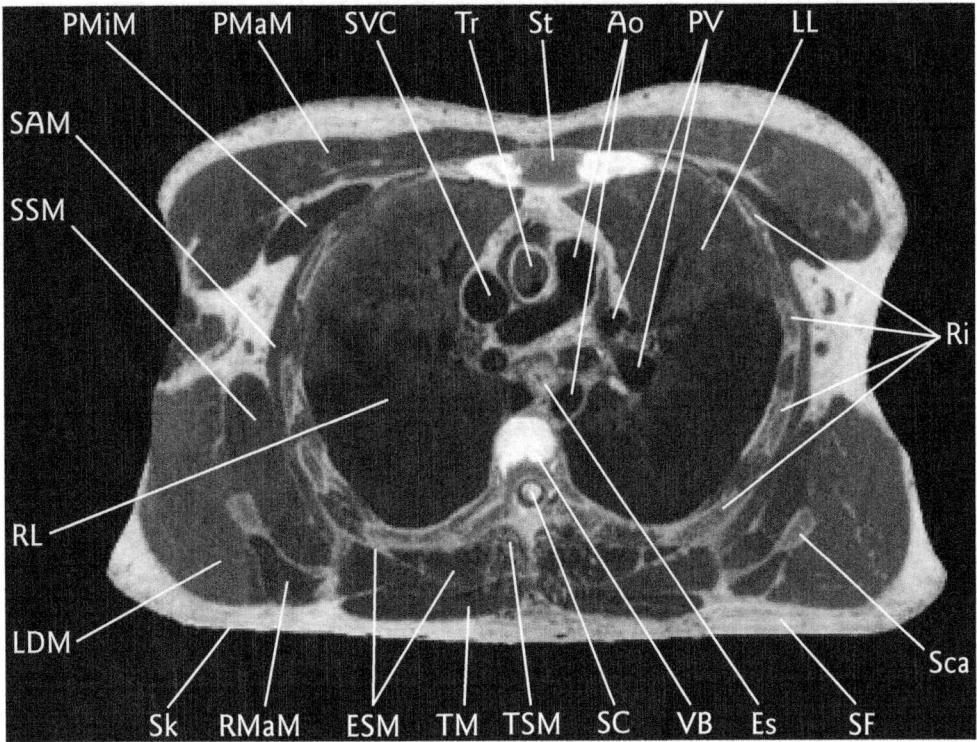

Figure 13: *Chiwari*. Structures encountered —

Ao: aorta
ESM: erector spinae muscles
LL: left lung
PMiM: pectoralis minor muscle
Ri: ribs
RMaM: rhomboid major muscle
SC: spinal canal
SF: subcutaneous fat
SSM: subscapularis muscle
SVC: superior vena cava
Tr: trachea
VB: vertebral body

Es: esophagus
LDM: latissimus dorsi muscle
PMaM: pectoralis major muscle
PV: pulmonary vessels
RL: right lung
SAM: serratus anterior muscle
Sca: scapula
Sk: skin
St: sternum
TM: trapezius muscle
TSM: transversospinalis muscles

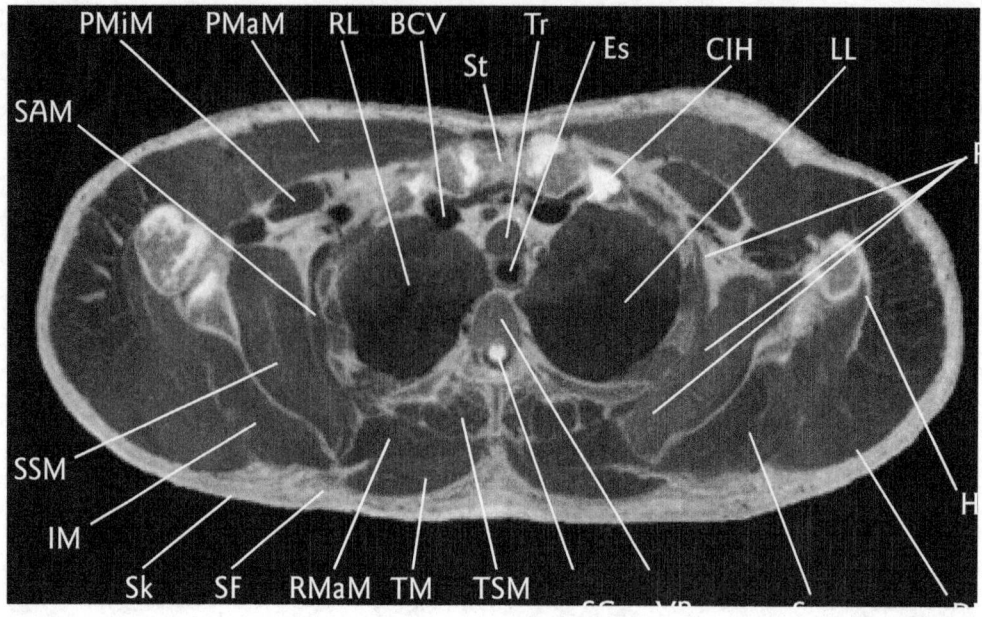

Figure 14: *Karigane.* Structures encountered —
BCV: brachiocephalic vessels
ClH: clavicular head
DM: deltoid muscle
Es: esophagus
Hu: humerus
IM: infraspinatus muscle
LL: left lung
PMaM: pectoralis major muscle
PMiM: pectoralis minor muscle
Ri: ribs
RL: right lung
RMaM: rhomboid major muscle
SAM: serratus anterior muscle
SC: spinal canal
Sca: scapula
SF: subcutaneous fat
Sk: skin
SSM: subscapularis muscle
St: sternum
TM: trapezius muscle
Tr: trachea
TSM: transversospinalis muscles
VB: vertebral body

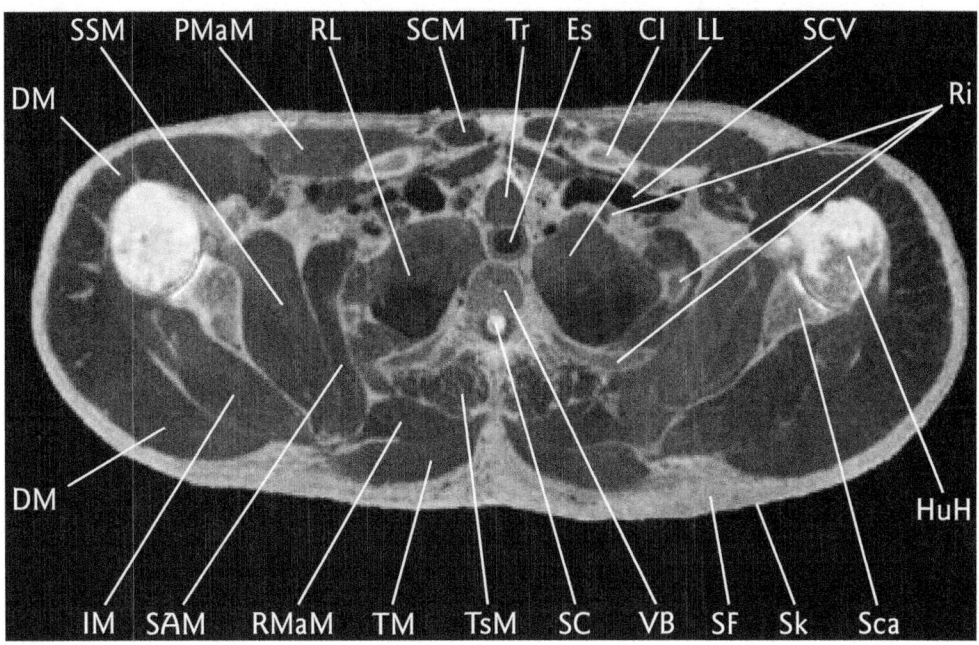

Figure 15: *Taitai*. Structures encountered —
    Cl: clavicle
    DM: deltoid muscle
    Es: esophagus
    HuH: humeral head
    IM: infraspinatus muscle
    LL: left lungs
    PMaM: pectoralis major muscle
    Ri: ribs
    RL: right lung
    RMaM: rhomboid major muscle
    SAM: serratus anterior muscle
    SC: spinal canal
    Sca: scapula
    SCM: sternocleidomastoid muscle
    SCV: subclavian vessels
    SF: subcutaneous fat
    Sk: skin
    SSM: subscapularis muscle
    TM: trapezius muscle
    Tr: trachea
    TSM: transversospinalis muscles
    VB: vertebral body

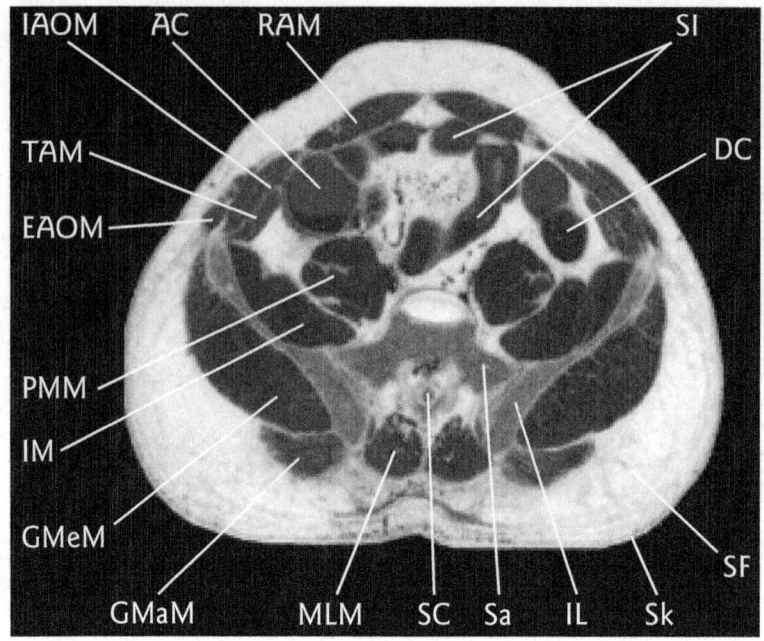

Figure 16: *Ryo kuruma*. Structures encountered —
AC: ascending colon
DC: descending colon
EAOM: external abdominal oblique muscle
GMaM: gluteus maximus muscle
GMeM: gluteus medius muscle
IAOM: internal abdominal oblique muscle
IL: ilium
IM: iliacus muscle
MLM: multifidis lumborum muscle
PMM: psoas major muscle
RAM: rectus abdominis muscle
Sa: sacrum
SC: spinal canal
SI: small intestines
SF: subcutaneous fat
Ski: skin
TAM: transversus abdominis muscle

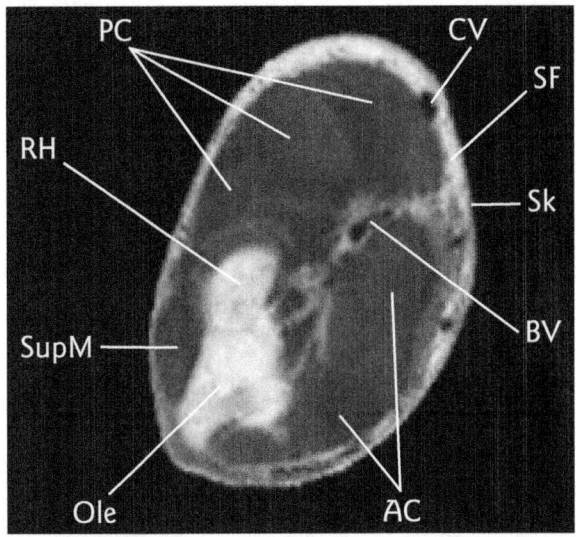

Figure 17: *Hiji.*
Structures encountered —
- AC: anterior compartment of forearm
- BV: brachial vessels
- CV: cephalic vein
- Ole: olecranon process of ulna
- PC: posterior compartment of forearm
- RH: radial head
- SF: subcutaneous fat
- Sk: skin
- SupM: supinator muscle

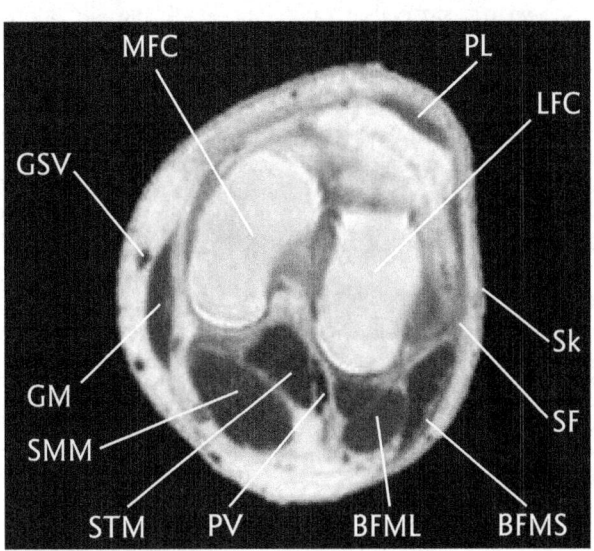

Figure 18: *Hizaguchi.* Structures encountered —
- BML: biceps femoris muscle, long head
- BMS: biceps femoris muscle, short head
- GM: gracilis muscle
- GSV: greater saphenous vein
- LFC: lateral femoral condyle
- MFC: medial femoral condyle
- PL: patellar ligament
- PV: popliteal vessels
- SF: subcutaneous fat
- Sk: skin
- SMM: semimembranosus muscle
- STM: semitendinosus muscle

Concluding Remarks

Tameshigiri cuts that were listed as difficult were thick and had a significant amount of bony tissue. This makes intuitive sense, since thicker targets have more tissue to impede the sword, and bone can deflect a blade. The mystique that has grown around the samurai swords in popular culture obscures the fact that these blades are not able to effortlessly cleave people in half. A forensic review of samurai bones from the Zaimokuza battlefield shows that even these feudal warriors were unable to consistently make clean cuts through their opponents. Evidence of bony deflection and "skipping" of a blade across tissues was found repeatedly (Karasulas, 2004). While these deflected cuts would still have been associated with massive soft-tissue trauma, it is clear that practices like tameshigiri were necessarily intended to sharpen the skill of those involved.

As the tameshigiri use of enemy combatants or executed criminals waned, inanimate objects took their place. It is still common practice in many kenjutsu (combative study of the Japanese sword) schools to cut rice stalk bales soaked with water and wrapped around a bamboo pole to mimic a limb. Even in this process it takes practice to deliver a clean cut that is not deflected by the bamboo within the target (Karasulas, 2004). The tameshigiri cuts that replicate the difficulty of these sorts of cuts are hizaguchi, hiji, sodesuri, and tabigata. The Yamada family considered these to be relatively simple in comparison to the cuts that passed through a larger cross section of the body. The most difficult cuts, ryo kuruma and tai-tai, involve cleaving through a large section of the body with a significant core of dense bone. The irregular shape of these bones may also make a clean cut exceedingly difficult.

Much as the samurai class lost interest in the practice of tameshigiri on the bodies of executed criminals, modern readers may find this to be a brutal and grotesque practice. Apart from the unavoidable gore, the idea of destroying a human body in such a manner is repugnant to many. Because the bodies of condemned criminals were used during these sessions, tameshigiri was also seen as an additional punishment to the criminal, since his body could no longer be properly buried. Samurai, clergy, women, and those with visible skin conditions were typically exempted.

Before delivering a verdict on the morality of this practice, modern readers should place tameshigiri into its proper historical and cultural context. Unlike anatomical dissection, the purpose of this practice was not an understanding of the human body for education or discovery. It was intended to test the ability of swords and swordsmen to cut effectively in a militarized and violent time. While this practice might have been a preface to a more modern understanding of human anatomy, this development did not occur. Instead, the social pressures in historical Japan pushed the development of tameshigiri to become a way of measuring the prestige of a hand-forged blade. A modern appreciation of scientific anatomy was ushered in with the Meiji Restoration of 1868, the same time as tameshigiri of corpses ceased and Japan entered a period of intense modernization.

Acknowledgments

I would like to thank the National Library of Medicine and the Visible Human Project for creating the images and data at the heart of this project. This would have been impossible without Professor R.D. Hersch and team of the Ecole Polytechnique Fédérale de Lausanne (EPFL). Switzerland, who developed the Visible Human viewer and have made it available for use in scientific investigations. More important, I would like to acknowledge the visual male himself, Joseph Paul Jernigan.

References

Berenson, A. (2005, October 15). Lipitor or generic? Billion-dollar battle looms. New York Times. Also found at http://www.nytimes.com/ 2005/10/15/business/15statin.html?pagewanted=all.

Joly, H., & Hogitaro, I. (1963) *The sword and same*. Boston: Charles Tuttle.

Karasulas, A. (2004). Zaimokuza reconsidered: The forensic evidence and classical Japanese swordsmanship. *World archaeology*, 36(4), 507–518.

Kremer, C., Racette, S., Schellenberg, M., Chaltchi, A., & Sauvageau, A. (2008). *American Journal of Forensic Medicine and Pathology*, 29(1), 5–8.

Takeuchi, S. (2009). Tameshigiri (and suemonogiri) as a sub-cultural custom and social structure in feudal era Japan: A socio-cultural analysis of transformation of its symbolic meanings and functions. *Asian Social Science*, 5 (11), 3–14.

Visible Human Slice Viewer. Courtesy Prof. R. Hersch, Ecole Polytechnique Federale de Lausanne (EPFL), Switzerland, Visible Human Web Server http://visiblehuman.epfl.ch. Accessed December 1, 2011.

The Ainu and Their Swords in Japan: A Concise Overview
by Curt Peritz

In this photograph an Ainu couple pose dressed in clothing representative of their culture. The sword, hung by a sash over the husband's shoulder, also exhibits a stylistic Ainu design. Photo courtesy of the Peabody Museum.

Introduction

Many have heard of the heroic and romantic stories associated with Japanese history, particularly of the famous samurai. In works of art, plays, books and films, the samurai are commemorated for all time. Very little, however, is known of their early adversaries who have lived in Japan for millennia and retreated as a dwindling minority to the far north. This essay is the result of many years of study and research into one special aspect of the fascinating people of northern Japan: the Ainu.

As a chapter title, "The Ainu and Their Swords in Japan" is fully justified in the light of the historical events of the last two thousand years. It is now generally accepted that the Ainu have lived for over seven thousand years in many areas of Japan, even as far south as the island of Kyushu near Hiroshima and to the far north beyond Sakhalin (*Karafuto*).

They came from eastern Siberia and are related to Caucasian tribes whose population had expanded into these vast, lonely lands, following the rivers to the seashore to hunt and fish. They were called the "hairy Ainu," since a hirsute appearance is one of the characteristics of the men as well as their white skin. The tools and weapons used by the Ainu were almost identical to those used all over the world at that time. Metal came into use in the ancient Middle East about four thousand years ago and its use spread. The colder regions of the world had metal quite late, often far less than one thousand years ago. The tools of the Eskimo and the Ainu, for example, were almost identical according to their corresponding type and usage. The main material they had used for making tools and weapons was wood, a craft with which the Ainu were experts. The Australian aborigines also only had a wood, shell, bone and stone culture until very recently.

During the late Jomon and early Yayoi periods (cir. 2,000 to 100 BCE), Ainu society had evolved into cohesive communities (Utar). Other groups immigrated into the areas where the Ainu had settled in Japan. Serious armed conflicts began and, over time, increased in frequency and ferocity. The new immigrants, including the Asian mainland Okhotsk people, were contesting for living space. The Ainu had to fight for centuries but were slowly forced to give up ground everywhere except in Northern Honshu where they held on to much territory.

The Ainu heroic *epos yukar* were poetic and sing-song renderings of these historic incidents and were told and recited from generation to generation. The Ainu have no written language but their hundreds of art symbols express some of their thoughts ranging from the most mundane matters to aspects of religion, mysticism, and clan markings.

During the wars in Japan with the Yamato people, the Ainu had no metal weapons and used what they could capture, buy, or trade. They were known as fierce fighters and their excellence as great hunters must have helped, especially when using poison-tipped arrows with their short Asiatic bows.

In 1700 CE, there lived the venerable scholar named Arai Hakuseki, the first to describe an Ainu sword in his book *The Sword and Same*. Since then, Ainu weaponry has barely been mentioned in the West and is a rare topic even in Japan. As a result, facts about the Ainu sword remain unclear. With this chapter, I hope to clarify some important aspects regarding the Ainu and their swords.

Ainu men posing with their weapons.
Photo courtesy of the Peabody Museum.

An Analytical Study

Experts still debate the exact period when the Ainu began to settle more than half of the area comprising modern Japan, but most agree that it occurred between seven and ten thousand years ago. They came from the extreme northeast of the Asian mainland and lived as hunters and gatherers very much like the Eskimo further north. The similarity ends there; the Ainu belonging to a very different racial strain, more akin to the early Siberian people migrating from the West. In the dawn of humanity, migration was the way of life for people in search of food and better living conditions for the family and the group in which they lived. Harsh climatic conditions influenced the life styles of these people and forced them eventually to migrate.

The early ancestors of the Ainu may not have looked exactly like the Ainu of today. Because of their outstanding feature, a hirsute appearance, they were known as the "hairy Ainu." Their facial features were more Caucasian than Asiatic, but after many millennia changes have appeared owing to gradual intermarriage with Asiatic peoples in that area.

The Ainu lived as hunters, fishermen and gatherers, mainly in the coastal areas of Japan from beyond the north of Japan and Hokkaido, and as far south as the Shikoku Island. During the pre-historic era, when the Yayoi period began (cir. 250 BCE), artifacts show the Ainu continuing to live in the simplest manner. As yet, there was no knowledge of metal manufacture of any kind.

The usual materials for weapon making at this primitive level of culture were flint, bone, and pointed and hardened wood. When copper and bronze finally emerged, soon followed by iron, the Ainu did not accept these new materials because of their rarity and the Ainu's lack of knowledge of how to work them.

The Ainu experienced early conflicts with other people who also settled into the lands of Shikoku, Kyushu and Honshu. These were primarily clashes between groups of hunters who utilized poisoned arrows. In later conflicts, both sides began to use bows and arrows and primitive bronze and iron swords of the early *ken* type. These clashes became more frequent and the Ainu gained a reputation as fierce fighters despite their primitive weaponry. During the Yayoi Period (cir. 250 BCE to 300 CE), people in Japan began to develop contacts with mainland China and Korea. The ever important arms production, even in these early times, began to grow and artisans arrived to help it develop. Metalworkers and swordsmiths from China passed on their knowledge to people willing to learn. Soon the pupils were becoming skilled and a specialized metal-weapons industry came into being.

Ainu Heroes

In the seventh century, the Ainu defeated the Okhotsk, an enemy whom they referred to as the "Sea People" (*Reunpur*). The Ainu called themselves *Yaunkur*, or "Land People." The famous hero of this early war was named Poiyaunpe, meaning "young mainlander." In 1456–57, the Ainu hero Koshamain was defeated in battle by Takeda Nobuhiro. This eventually lead to the Ainus' submission to the Japanese.

After the Kofun era ended in 552 CE, there emerged several good short, medium and long swords. These included the short *ken* with a tongue shaped double-edged blade, the short sword or *musoto*, the medium long *kanto tsurugi*, and a straight sword with one edge made of bronze or iron. Another sword which came into being and is shown on some Haniwa clay figures was the *warabite tachi*, which would prove to have a lasting presence in Japanese history.

It must be noted that during the years between 552 and 700 CE, more famous swords emerged: all of them were straight; most were one-edged; all were tachi, worn cutting edge down in their suspension.

The Ainu living in Japan during that early period could only obtain swords

Photo courtesy of the Peabody Museum.

by means of war booty or by barter. There is no doubt that the Ainu would use any sword they could obtain. Furthermore, the religious beliefs and attitudes they had would enhance the importance of any sword coming into their possession. This attitude has not changed since these ancient times. It may have even deepened.

The bitter skirmishes between the Japanese armed forces and the Ainu became fiercer and more protracted. It is easy to visualize the Ainu in those far off days waging a sort of jungle warfare, since as hunters they were masters at concealment and ambush tactics. In an illustration in *The Sword and the Same*, a group of four Ainu warriors is depicted carrying long tachi on their backs, the hilt protruding over the left shoulder. These are obviously captured tachi used in warfare. These swords, being curved tachi, date the scene to approximately 1350. There is another illustration in Hakuseki's book showing a typical Ainu sword of that time. The sword is named *emush* in the Ainu.

Other words relating to swords are common in the Ainu language. For example, a sword given to an Ainu chieftain as a sign of honorary recognition is called *ibetam*. One can presume care was taken to keep such a sword in its original condition. The name *magiri* actually refers to a short utility sword-knife. There is also a small knife called *ikoro*, which is an insignia for a chief of the Mukawa area on Hokkaido.

As mentioned above, most swords which the Ainu obtained were soon altered to suit the religious practices and ideology of these people. The emushi sword shown in Hakuseki's book, which has the proportions of a large *wakizashi*, is illustrated as being held by a broad sash draped over one shoulder. This sash has great importance to the Ainu. It is made of natural fibers, including prepared elm bark, woven by elected women who have some shamanistic standing in the community. A small upright loom is used for this work. Mystical and religious powers are ascribed to the sash itself. The sword and sash together are also the mainstay of the ceremonial sword dance (*emush-remuse*), which was performed up into the 1950's in a simplified version for tourists visiting Hokkaido.

The importance of the sword and sash have never lessened but are held sacred to the Ainu themselves even today. An illustration from Hakuseki's book showing an elderly white haired Ainu with three black-bearded younger men—all carrying tachi on their backs—reappears early this century in a Hokkaido Tourist Agency publication.

Battles in the early Heian Era (794–1185 CE) drove the Ainu northward from central Japan, particularly after Sei-i Tai-Shogun Sakanoue Tamura Maro (758–811 CE) took charge of the campaign. The Ainu were defeated by larger numbers of better-armed soldiers and so retreated to Hokkaido in a large exodus. There is no epic describing these momentous events. Following the exodus, the Ainu must have retreated even more into their spiritual life and religious customs in greater secrecy and seclusion.

The protracted campaign to make the Ainu retreat from more than half of Honshu and other places was still fought with the straight-bladed sword of the single-edge type called *chokuto* and *tsurugi* as well as a ring-pommelled kind of sword (*kanto tachi*) and an egg-pommelled type (*kabutsuchi no tachi*). These early sword types were of Korean origin.

Historically this was still the era of the straight sword in Japan. The first truly curved tachi did not become known until the beginning of the ninth century. The mysterious appearance of the slightly curved *kogarasumaru*, accredited to one swordsmith named Amakuni, cannot be exactly dated. Almost immediately after it there appeared the even more mysterious sword *kenukigata*, whose originators are unknown, but which could be found in the records of early swordsmiths and who date its appearance between the late ninth century and the late tenth century.

Finally, truly curved swords were made in Japan during the ninth century in the perfect form made by Yasutsun of Hoki and his son. There were magnificent swords known in Japan previously, such as the *kogarasumaru* and the *kenukigata*, both partly curved. There was also a group of curved swords exemplified by the arrival of a fashion in Chinese and Korean tachi which made their appearance in the time of Prince Shotoku (547–622 CE).

At first, these too were straight, but gradually developed into a curved blade. However gradual the change from straight to curved, the *kogarasuemaru* and the *kenukigata* illustrate the beginning of curved swords in Japan. The former short *warabite no tachi* became longer and stronger and was used in battle with the Ainu, finally becoming known as the *kurotsukuri no tachi* (black sword). This kind of sword finally heralded the end of the straight tachi. There was of course an intermediate period in which any type of sword available was used when conflicts broke out.

The Ainu, facing such a high quality and overwhelming abundance of arms used by the Japanese, had to retreat and finally come to terms with their subjugation. Even in the following centuries, the Ainu never did become swordsmiths or even metalworkers. Wood was their chief material and in it they were experts.

In the last eighteen hundred years, they probably gathered many thousands of swords which were given an elevated status far beyond that of trophies. The swords were possibly sanctified and, of course, purified to become holy relics. Damaged swords were stripped and their parts used in the making of new, "reborn" Ainu-style swords with a totally different exterior and multiple carvings all beautifully done.

The Ainu craft of wood carving has so advanced that an uninitiated person can not tell a real sword from one they have fully replicated in wood. These sacred Ainu emushi have metallic-looking *kashira* or *kabutogane*. As the sword types may be mixed, so are the fittings, also carved realistically.

The standard emushi used by the Ainu in ceremonies is very similar to the one found in Hakuseki's *Sword and the Same*. It seems, in fact, to be a version of a broad wakizashi suspended in the loops of the sacred sash (*atsu*) and almost always beautifully carved with rolling waves, geometric patterns, or plants. Many have pointed pommels, as illustrated after the next few paragraphs.

On quite a select number of swords, the area between the front and rear loop of the sash has an object attached at the omote side. This object usually is the most important carved spatula, stick or wand called *ikui-bashui*. It is used to sprinkle or fling drops of sake from the cup, just before it is drunk as a gesture of blessing and libation. That this spatula may also be helpful in pushing the beard aside while eating or drinking is incidental. This ikui-bashui is almost always carved with some dominating motif.

As a sign of extra honor, a smaller secondary sword might be worn attached to the omote side of the sword. The Ainu have several styles of swords of varying dimensions and quality. The more swords an Ainu owns, it is believed, the greater his social standing.

The Japanese sentiment about the quality of a sword's blade or its maker is of little or no importance to an Ainu. One may assume that some rudimentary care is taken of these swords, but as far as could be gathered, no ritualistic maintenance exists.

There are four main types of Ainu swords: tachi, katana, uchie and chisaagatana, and wakizashi. Some tanto may be included as an additional type. As in olden days, all of these types of swords were made for the purpose of warfare. Those which were partially or totally stripped sometime in their history and "reborn" according to Ainu style were also for war. Those which were remodelled for ceremonial uses and those which were perfect replicas were made totally in wood. The pommels of 60–70% of swords were pointed as shown below. The pointed pommel represents the "Bird God" (*Chika Kanui*).

A Typical Ainu Sword

This is a typical Ainu sword called an *emushi*. If it has a sash in which it is carried, then it is called *emuchi atsu* (pronounced *emushatt*). The weaving of special sashes for these swords was done by elected female shamans who held high social position. The swords and sashes were given magic powers and became talimans or protective objects in ritualistic activities and emushi-emuse dances. These swords are rarely seen today except in tourism-sponsored activities.

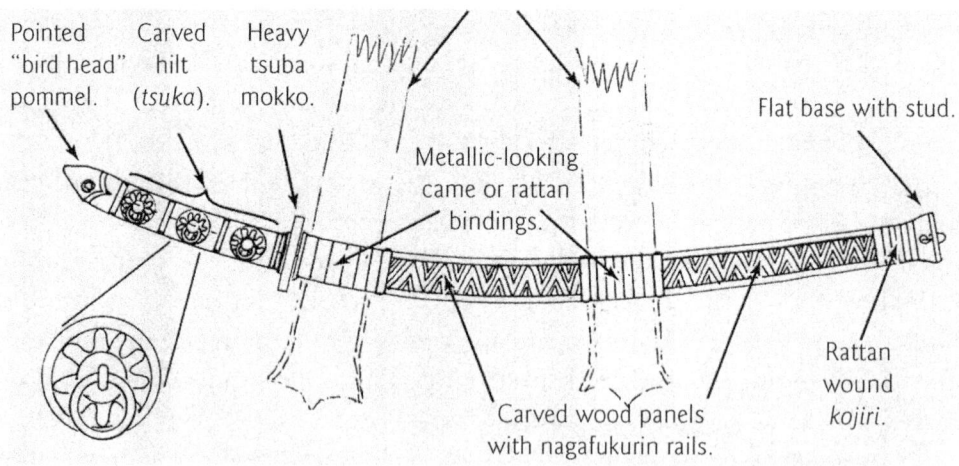

Front side of the sash (*atsu*). The rear part of the sash has the same pattern as the front. It lies over the top of the right shoulder of the wearer.

Details of a hilt ornament with moveable rings for tassels.
(Design used in Korea since 200 BCE).

Overall length: 95cm (37-3/8")
Hilt: 25cm (9-7/8")
All drawings by C. Peritz.

Typical Ainu Sword-Knife
top-view of scabbard.

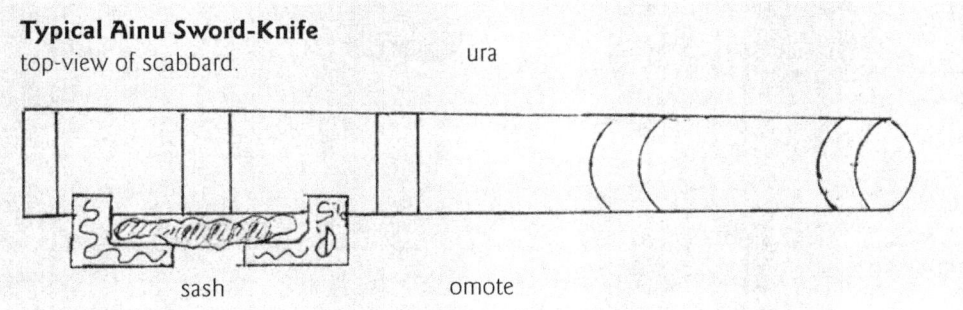

Typical Ainu Sword-Knife
Lateral view of the scabbard showing the hook-clips from above.

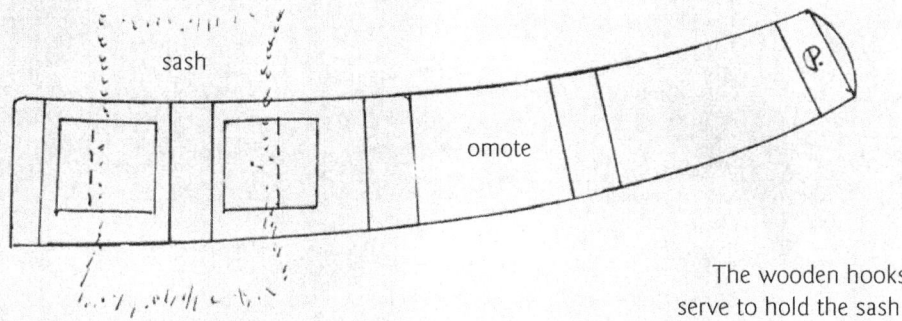

The wooden hooks serve to hold the sash.

Typical Ainu Sword-Knife
Average length: 20"

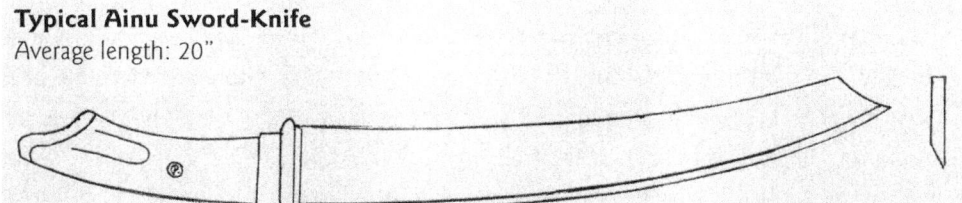

This is a *tashiro* of the *kata kiri ba* style having a blade sharpened on one edge only.

Description of Eight Ainu Swords

1) This sword is known as an *efu tachi*. Its overall length is approximately 100 cm long. This tachi has a so-called *shitogi tsuba* with extra guard rings called *kutsura gane*. The sword was partially stripped of its former fittings, which were replaced by Ainu-styled *kanagu*. The *kabuto gane* and *ishizuke* were still in place, but the hilt surfaces were bared. The main body of the scabbard had a set of large seme-rings with the special decor sash. A cord is attached to its *ashi-kanamono*. No information is available on the blade. The hilt also retains its original Japanese tassel a well as a set of eight *tawara-byo* tang location pins and a display of real or carved *nagafukurin* rails along the top and underside of the scabbard.

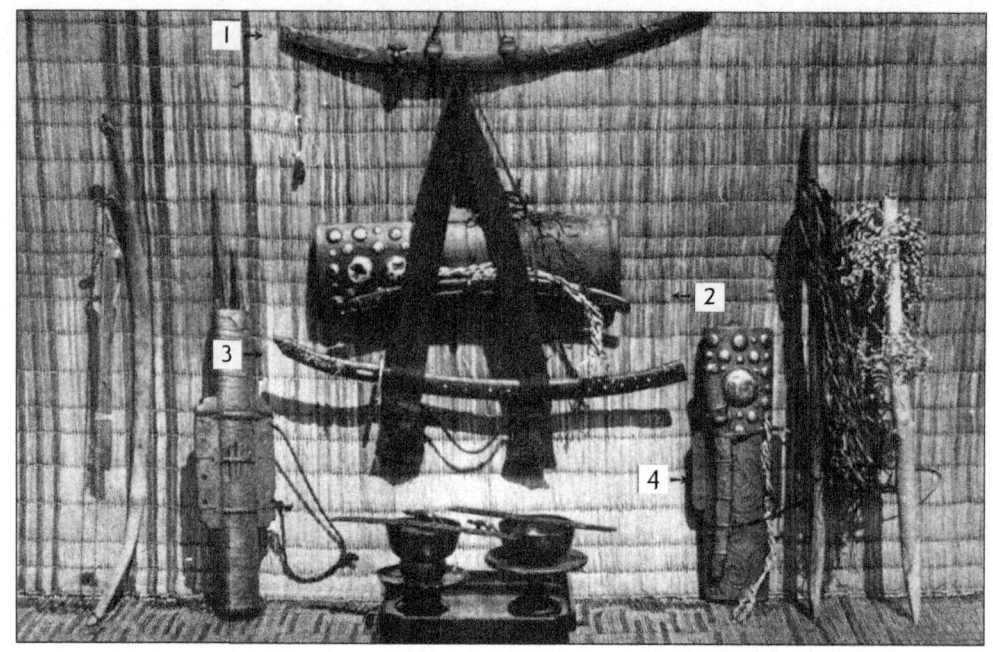

Ainu swords and hunting gear.
"Moustache wands" (*ikui-bashui*) rest on the drinking vessels.
Photo courtesy of the Peabody Museum.

2) This is an old court sword used for war. This is a shorter sword, possibly a wakizashi, refitted to Ainu ceremonial requirements. It is 75 cm in total length with a hilt of 18 cm. It is suspended by cords worn around the waist or, as with a sash, by a cord placed over the shoulder. The blade is possibly of the *kata kiri ba* style or of the *hira zukuri* shape.

3) This sword seemed to have been a former tachi. Its overall length is 95 cm; its hilt, 30 cm. It could also have been a katana or uchi-gatana many of which have been made. The Ainu way of redecorating such a sword unintentionally disguises its original features. The approximate measurements could fit either a tachi, a katana or an uchi-gatana. No information is available on the blade. The hilt has been severely reshaped and the scabbard has received the full Ainu restyling. As a major feature, the restyling includes the alteration of the *kojiri* or *ishizuke* of the sword, depending on which type of sword it is. This Ainu styling of the kojiri is a standard procedure on most converted swords and goes hand in hand with the use of the pointed *kashira* or *kabuto gane*. The reason behind these shapes and carvings must be sought in the art history of the Ainu.

4) Unfortunately, this is only a remnant of a typical Ainu short sword of the dimension of a wakizashi. Now all that remains is the scabbard which displays a set of four seme between a finely shaped *kojiri* and the upper *koi guchi* of an unusual scabbard measuring 50 cm in overall length.

Group of Ainu men.
Photo courtesy of the Peabody Museum.

5) This is a tachi, 100 cm in overall length with a hilt of 25 cm. This sword is wrapped in cord netting and worn in a sash. No information is available on the blade.
6) This is a tachi in the sash that has similar dimensions as given in description No. 1 on this page. Here too the scabbard and hilt are bound with heavy cords in net style.
7) This sword is an *itomaki-no-tachi* of similar dimensions to the preceding. It is worn in a sash over the right shoulder. The *tsuba* is of the Aoi style, and again the scabbard and hilt are wrapped in netting cord. The blade was made for war by an unknown smith.
8) This is a *ko-dachi* style sword. Its overall length is 80 cm; its hilt is 20 cm. It is wrapped and bound with cords in a fish-net style on hilt and scabbard. It is suspended by cords and a thin sash over the left shoulder. The tsuba is small and indistinct (*uchi-gatana*). The blade may be of iron in the *kata kiri ba* shape.

Concluding Remarks on the List of Ainu Swords

The Ainu swords described here came into fashion during the advent of the curved sword in Japan in the late Heian period, roughly a thousand years ago. The name emushi may have appeared only when the curved Japanese tachi made their appearance. The age of the emushi swords may vary considerably. The Ainu, being understandably very secretive about their own history, could keep records only by word of mouth. There is no written Ainu language. There is an explanation, however, for the design alterations on former Japanese swords. The fact remains that most of these swords are altered to suit the Ainu concepts for clan patterns and artistic design. There is no doubt that most swords would have been used in war, whenever available. It is also possible that swords for war were not altered or only altered slightly. This is the case with most long tachi or uchi-gatana and katana. The wakizashi style of sword is preferred much in later, more peaceful times and this style may have dominated the preference of sword-carrying Ainu chieftains and men. Swords have played a major part in Ainu religion and ceremonies as well as in dances called *emushi–remuse*. As with the samurai, a status no Ainu could ever aspire to attain, the sword was an item of sacred import and reverence, a token of personal honor and respect for a tranquil and serene world in harmony with nature.

The acquisition of more than one sword raised the status of the proud owner and, as with the Japanese people, became a treasure. The habit of adding another knife or other implements to the side of a sword scabbard was adopted from the Japanese katana and wakizashi. On the scabbard were added the *kozuka* or the *kogai* or even two chopsticks. On the Ainu's sword scabbard, it may have been the miniature sword or a similarly styled libation-wand called *ikui-bashui* used during the drinking of sake. It was called "moustache lifting stick" by the Japanese. The possibility exists that other items may be carried in that manner. The all important sash (*atsu*), for instance, has pockets for such purposes. The blades in Ainu swords were of Japanese make and little attention or care was given to the quality of such a blade.

Swords carried by the Ainu through the centuries have exhibited the uniqueness of their culture—aesthetically presenting their political, social, and religious beliefs. It is the desire of this author that this chapter will add to the understanding of the Ainu and their swords. Hopefully, others will choose to continue research into this fascinating subject before the Ainu culture becomes more obscured as a relic of antiquity trapped in a modernizing world.

Glossary

- *Apniniap:* Double-pointed salmon spear.
- *Attsu:* The sash for carrying the Ainu tachi, woven by Ainu women of shamanistic standing in the community. Derives from the word *attuch*.
- *Attush:* Fabric from the inner bark of the mountain elm (*Atni*; Latin, *ulmus laciniata*), which is boiled and then chewed and dyed. Woven on an erect loom.
- *Emushi:* Sword. In combination with the sash, it is called *emush-att*.
- *Ibetam:* A Japanese sword given to the Ainu by an official as token of recognition, *tam* being the ancient rood word for "sword."
- *Ibe-bashui:* Wand or a pair of sticks for touching hot food, i.e., chopsticks, sometimes worn on the outer side of an Ainu scabbard, very much like the *kogai* and *kozuka* of the samurai sword where chopsticks were sometimes placed.
- *Ika*, or *ikayop*: Quiver for arrows.
- *Ikoro:* A small knife. An insignia of a leader of a group-settlement "possession" (*kotan*). This knife may have been affixed to the omote side of a scabbard very much like the kozuka in the katana.
- *Ikui-bashui:* The ritual libation wand often called *higebera* (moustache-lifters) by the Japanese. Often attached to the outer side of the scabbard.
- *Itoppa:* A knife of insignia of ownership, sometimes personalized.
- *Magiri*, or *magirihi*: Early word for "sword," or "sword-knife."
- *Marek:* Single-pointed salmon spear.
- *Nishpa:* A chieftain or boss.
- *Repni:* Carved or plain ceremonial sticks used percussively to sound out rhythms during recitals.
- *Sexpa*, or *sechpa*: Sword guard (jap. *tsuba*).
- *Stomusi:* Buckle or gird on a sword.
- *Tam:* "Sword" when used in conjunction with other words.
- *Tamambe:* Long sword.
- *Tasiro*, or *tashiro*: Long knife.
- *Tomi*, or *tomine*: "Precious thing," referring to a sword.

Special Thanks
To the Peabody Essex Museum
for the use of all the photographs
used to illustrate this chapter
and in particular to
Kathy Flynn (photography department)
and Mark Sexton (staff photographer)
for their kind help.

Bibliography

Aston, W. (1972). *Nihongi*. Tokyo: Charles E. Tuttle, Co.

Batchelor, J. (1891). *The Ainu of Japan*. New York: Fleming H. Revell Co.

Batchelor, J. (1901). *The Ainu and their folk lore*. London: The Religious Tract Society. Also the 1967 reprint by Univeristy Microfilms International, Ann Arbor, Michigan.

Bird, I. (1971). *Unbeaten tracks in Japan*. Tokyo: Charles E. Tuttle, Co.

British Museum. (n.d.). *British museum booklet on the Ainu*. London: British Museum.

Bushell, R. (1964). *Wonderful world of netsuke*. Tokyo: Charles E. Tuttle, Co.

Craig-McCullogh, H. (1979). *Taiheiki*. Tokyo: Charles E. Tuttle, Co.

Czaplicka, M. (1914). *Aboriginal Siberia*. Oxford: Clarendon Press.

Draeger, D., & Smith, R. (1969). *Asian fighting arts*. New York: Kodansha International.

Haruseki, A. (1988). *Sword and the same*. (H. Joly, and H. Inada, Trans.) England: New Holland Publishing (Original work published in 1700).

Hawley, W. (1981). *Japanese swordsmiths*. Hollywood, CA: Hawley Publications. Revised edition.

Hepburn, J. (1983). *Japanese and English dictionary*. Rutland, VT: Charles E. Tuttle, Co.

Hilger, M. (1971). *Together with the Ainu*. Norman, Oklahoma: University of Oklahoma Press.

Kidder, E. (1959). *Japan before Buddhism*. London: Thames & Hudson; with, Norwich: Jarrold and Sons, Ltd.

Morse, E. (1990). *Japan day by day*. Atlanta, GA: Cherokee Publishing Co. (Original work published in 1877).

Munro, N. (1962). *Ainu creed and cult*. London: Routledge & Kegan Paul, Ltd.

Ozaki, Y. (1975). *Japanese fairy book*. Rutland, VT: Charles E. Tuttle, Co.

Papinot, E. (1972). *Historical and geographical dictionary of Japan*. Rutland, VT: Charles E. Tuttle, Co. (Original work published in French in 1910).

Phillippi, D. (1979). *Epic tradition of the Ainu: Song of God, song of man*. Tokyo: University of Tokyo Press.

Pike-Tay, A. (n.d.) Ainu artifacts. In *Mingei Japanese folk art*. Brooklyn, NY: Brooklyn Museum.

Pilsudski, B. (1912). *Materials for the study of the Ainu language and folklore*. Cracow, Poland: Imperial Academy of Sciences Spolka

Roberts, L. (1978). *Guide to Japans museum*. New York: Kodansha International.

Sadler, A. (1978). *Life of shogun Tokugawa Ieyasu*. Tokyo: Charles E. Tuttle, Co. (Original work published in 1937).

Savage Landor, A. (1893). *Alone with the hairy Ainu*. London: John Murray Publishers.

Slavik, A. (1952). *Die figentum marken der Ainu* [The property markings of the Ainu]. Berlin: Dietrich Reimer Verlag.

Stone, G. (1978). *Glossary of the construction, decor and use of arms and amour*. NY: Arms and Armour Press. (Original work published in 1934).

Takakura, S. (1960). *The Ainu of northern Japan*. Philadelphia: The American Philosophical Society.

Varley, P. (1980). *A syllabus of Japanese civilisation*. New York: Columbia University Press.

Yoshikawa, E. (1980). *The Heike story*. Tokyo: Charles E. Tuttle, Co. (Original work published in 1956).

1,000 Swordmaking Cuts: August Events at the Kingfisher Woodworks

by James Goedkoop, B.A.

Workshop
The author at work in the Kingfisher shop.

For Kingfisher WoodWorks, August is typically a slow month in the work year. Activity is low keyed and the demand for wooden swords and staffs is relaxed until cooler fall temperatures stimulate a resurgence of martial arts weapon practice in North American studios. Rather than having a negative effect on business, the August calm is a welcome cyclical event for Kingfisher. The slower pace of orders allows for attention to practical needs that were postponed during the year. New materials are tested, the wood inventory is replenished, and the shop is reorganized. Machinery is maintained and the array of specialized cutters is sharpened. There is a little breathing space for the development of ideas while the shop is preparing for the early fall and then the relentless pace of the busiest months, November through March.

The actual time of manufacture of samurai swords has historic significance. Some time ago, I came across the following reference regarding the preferred dating of Japanese swords: "Since no modern instruments were available to measure either the hardness or the temperature of steel, such factors were described by references to natural phenomena. For example, 'Heat the steel at final forging until it turns to the color of the moon about to set out on its journey across the heavens on a June or July evening' (old calendar); or, 'After the final forging, place the sword in water which has a temperature of water in February or August' (old calendar). They believed that water temperature in February and August was the same" (Yumoto, 1958: 97).

It is for this reason that many sword smiths made inscriptions certifying the date of their work in February or August and, to bring good fortune (in the market or otherwise), many blades undoubtedly produced at other times of the year also show a date of manufacture in these two months. What can be discerned from this strange statement, that the temperature of the water in a summer and a winter month is the same? Japan's latitude spans a similar range as the United States and has similar distinct seasons. Even taking into account the differences of the old calendar, February is a cold month and August is a hot month. To the modern reader, this cryptic explanation of water being the same temperature seems to be either some archaic logic whose reasoning has been lost over the centuries or one whose meaning is purposefully obscured.

While I don't date my work in a misleading way, over the years I've come to plan some projects so that when I discover a superb piece of wood, I'll begin work until I'm reasonably sure that it has ideal properties and then set it aside for completion the following August or February. Many of my reference works or wooden swords (*bokken*) that I've kept for personal reasons were produced in this manner. Water is not used in making wooden swords other than in sharpening the cutting tools that shape the wood and, unlike the quenching of steel, the water temperature has little bearing on woodworking. If I had to comment on an influential natural phenomenon, it is the quality of the daylight that fills the workshop, which is a factor that I think has a great influence on creativity. In an odd coincidence predating my awareness of the times of ideal water temperatures, I had discovered two times of year when the quality of light provides the best visual and atmospheric conditions for making wooden weapons: the warm orange glow of August and the opposed cold blue daylight of February.

The work of August 2002 was actually set up in June of that year. I had an unexpected call for work to be used in a film—a request for thirty wooden swords to be delivered by the end of August. They were to be typical in design of bokken made toward the end of the 19th century. This was the period of the collapse of

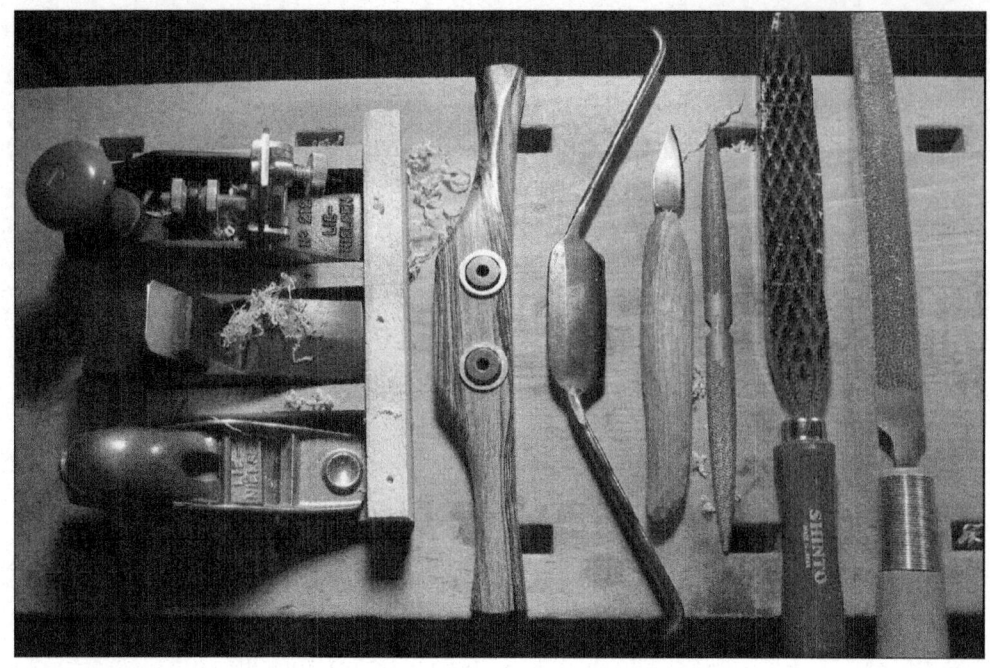

Handtools: Some of the tools used to shape the fine details of the weapons and create a cleanly cut surface.

the Japanese feudal system and the beginning of the so called Meiji Restoration. The film takes place during the time of the Satsuma Rebellion and the scene involves a practice session using wooden swords.

Japanese wooden swords of any period come in many variations and insofar as the set's art department wasn't specific as to the design or martial school (*ryu*) orientation, it was fairly easy to choose a couple of classic shapes with some typical stylistic variations. The planning of the project was routine and other than the fact that I needed to double my normal August production, only one nagging thought kept creeping up: woodworking made a huge transformation in the middle of the 20th century.

For one thing, machinery and factories were able to produce identical products quickly, but equally important, the advances in the quality of abrasives made it possible for a complete change in the finishing process as well. Most people now regard a smoothly sanded surface with high-quality finishing. Sanding is used primarily to remove machine marks, but sandpaper in general has developed so much so that abrasive belts and specialized machines are also frequently used for heavy stock removal. The use of abrasives is popular mainly because the heterogeneous nature of wood makes it so difficult to cut cleanly and smoothly. A relatively unskilled modern woodworker can produce a smooth surface by simply sanding with finer and finer grits of abrasives whereas in the past, a highly skilled woodworker cut extremely fine shavings from the surface, relying on the exceedingly sharp edges of a wide variety of specialized hand tools to produce a smooth surface.

Most people, even if they know nothing about woodworking, immediately recognize a poorly finished surface. There is evidence of machine marks visible, steps in the sanding process have been skipped and the work is usually covered with a synthetic looking finish. A good finish, by modern day standards, and one that has come to be regarded as the highest quality, is produced by thorough sanding and a combination of rubbing oils or varnishes. However, because the modern technique of sanding wood affects the wood differently than the methods of traditional work, the two, not surprisingly, produce a visual and tactile effect quite noticeably different.

A good sanded surface is actually inferior to a high quality cut surface. The shortcomings of sandpaper were immediately recognized by craftsmen fifty years ago, but as time rolled on, the financial advantages of sanding in the finishing process and the fact that sandpaper made woodworking more accessible to hobbyists, the drawbacks slipped out of common awareness.

Consider the sanding process itself: tiny bits of aluminum oxide or silicon carbide shred the wood fibers, grinding the wood down while driving dust and residual abrasive bits into the wood grain. No matter how fine the end step of sanding, the wood pores are already irreversibly clogged with contaminants. This was plainly evident to traditional craftsmen when they compared the sanded surface to the lively clean look of a surface planed with a razor sharp edge. In this case, cleanly severed wood fibers leave the pores wide open. The wood is able to deeply accept many applications of oil finish which can then be rubbed to a spectacular finish. The cleanly cut surface, finished with a hand rubbed oil, is better protected and is more beautiful than a sanded surface can ever become.

The procedure of sanding itself is not independently useful but exists, in a sense, as the handmaiden of the woodworking machine and adds to the dullness of the machine's execution. Consider, for example, that a machine must be set to perform a particular cut. Those settings cannot be changed in the middle of performing the cut. The machine follows the settings established by the operator but essentially governed by a program of the machine's designer. The machine can never transcend the limitations of itself and so the operator, no matter how inventive, always works within mechanical and practical boundaries that limited the mind of the designer. Evidence of these limits is not only the hallmark of modern woodworking but the hallmark of mass production as it relates to artistic expression. Compare, for a moment, the infinite flexibility of the hand and mind when performing brush calligraphy in contrast to the constraints imposed by a computer's drawing program.

Shave: A traditional style woodshave, made by the author, is used on the blade section of a wooden sword. This tool is sharpened and set to cut shavings only one or two thousandths of an inch thick and produces a glassy smooth surface. Hundreds of these little cuts make up the oval roundness and tapering sections of the sword.

No amount of technical sophistication can ever duplicate the artistic nuances of an unfettered human. A handheld cutting tool is like a brush in that the wrist and the infinite flexibility of the mind exists outside the geometrically conceived limitations of any program. Sanding, as it relates to woodworking, has come to simply be an extension of the woodworking machine and the work produced by a machine is dependent on the cosmetic action of sandpaper. Moreover, sanding is largely ineffective in adding value to the shape of the finished piece. It usually dulls finer features rather than enhancing them.

Some readers might compare the use of abrasives on wood with the abrasive techniques used in the polishing of a samurai sword. Metal, however, is physically completely different than wood and unlike wood, the use of abrasives on metal is not a technique of expedience but produces the most optimal finish.

These thoughts on the use of abrasives in woodwork have occupied my mind for many years. In the late 1980's, I started a transition from metal work to woodwork, and up until the mid-1990's, I worked almost exclusively in hard composite materials with properties more similar to metal than wood. In the late

1990's, I started to work primarily in natural hardwoods. Those materials, however, being oriented to the rigors of impact and sometimes abusive treatment, were extremely tough and difficult to work with using traditional methods. Despite several efforts, I was not able to produce reliably smooth surfaces with hand tools alone and like most other woodworkers, relied on modern abrasives.

So, the order for thirty bokken was placed in June 2002. The main requirement being that they represent work typical of 1876 Japanese craftsmanship. As I completed regular orders and tried to make room for this unexpected surge of work, the challenge I came to see was one entirely within myself. Had I not undertaken it, no one would have noticed anyway, I nevertheless committed myself to eliminating the use of sandpaper as it relates to the production of weapons made of natural wood. Now, without really thinking of the time of year, July quietly became August.

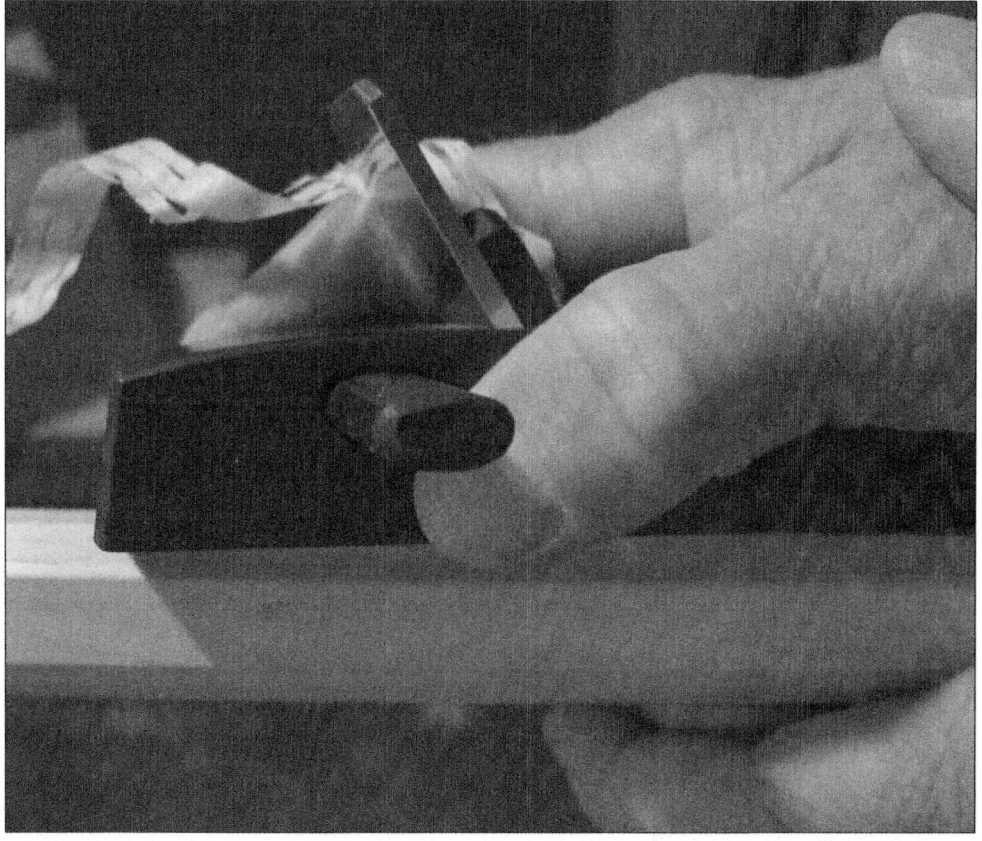

Plane: This wood bodied plane is set to cut the flat bevels on the back of the blade (*mune*). Notice the spiral shaving that floats up in front of the cutting edge. The blade on this tool must be exceedingly sharp.

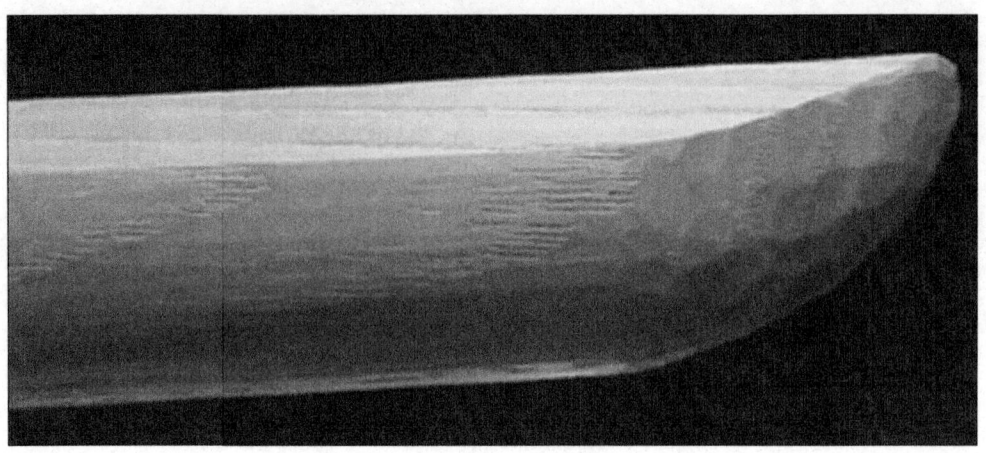

Kissaki: Small facets make up the point (*kissaki*) of this custom wooden sword. This picture, taken the following winter, shows how the blade section, although rounded, is actually defined by many, very small flat cuts. On the right, the blue light of a severely cold afternoon in early February reflects off the snow, through the window and highlights the edge.

As it turned out, I already had many pieces of this puzzle in place. The problem actually unraveled itself fairly quickly. Over the years I had acquired an assortment of planes, chisels and knives, both new and archaic. The only tool I bought now was a very small specialized wood-bodied hand plane that excelled at making extremely fine cuts.

It takes a long time to develop skill in sharpening these tools. An apprentice in a traditional Japanese wood shop spends two years sharpening tools before they commence with any woodwork. For all the hours I spent attempting to produce better and better edges over a period of time dating back to my youth, the only crucial difference between my earlier experiments and this effort was a simple but systematic approach of rearranging the dangling bits of knowledge of all those years. Without resorting to any expensive grinding machines, commercial jigs, fixtures, or esoteric sharpening systems, I found ways to hold the exact angles on the cutting edges and, equally important, create a simple but exact method of polishing those cutting edges without ruining the precise geometries of the bevels.

A sharp edge can be achieved in many ways and there are many opinions on how to achieve it, but this makes it no less difficult. For all the good sharpening methods, there are an infinite number of ways to create a dull edge. There is no mistaking a truly good edge. In the past, my hand tools were quite good. When carefully drawn against the skin as in a shaving motion, they could cut the hair off my arm. A really good edge, though, is uncommon. The safety net of sandpaper is readily available to erase any evidence of the imperfections. A really good edge

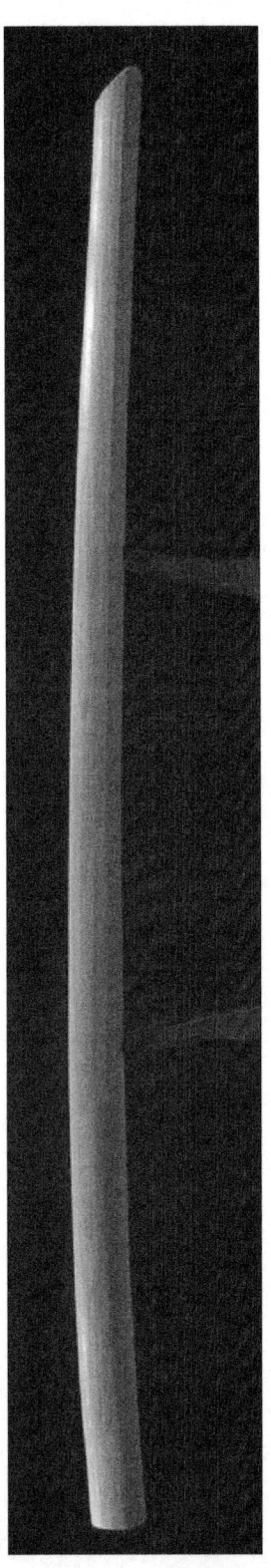

has the appearance of a mirror and it will shave hair perfectly and effortlessly very close to the skin. The steel backing the edge is substantial and thick enough to support it as it encounters the tough wood surface. Just like in a sword, the plane or chisel would lack the necessary mechanical strength of the shock it encounters without a perfect but stout backing of steel. It would dull quickly unless it had both perfect polish and geometry.

When everything is right, a good hand plane makes a kind of whispering, singing sound as it glides almost effortlessly through the wood. Paper thin curls of wood shavings spiral up in front of the cutting edge. The natural appearance of wood is a crisp, clear look that cannot be revealed any other way than by the action of a sharp-edged cutting tool.

The woodworker must rely on the physical action of cutting and, insofar as the production of traditional work requires countless motions of the body, the work must be achieved easily rather than through muscle strength or brute force. It is similar in the Japanese sword related martial arts. Devout students relentlessly practice to improve the quality of their strike rather than on the development of raw power. Countless swings teach the body to de-emphasize muscle strength of the arms and the dependence on the upper body yields to the vastly greater power of the body's core. One thousand sword cuts a day is a good amount. The arms fatigue quickly and, to continue, the well of power at the center must be engaged. It is not so different in other physical disciplines —huge amounts of wasted energy teach the body conservation. This path is traveled in any worthwhile skill. With practice, even a thousand cuts can be achieved with little fatigue.

Finished Bokken: Although simple in appearance, the Japanese wooden sword is a wonder of nuance, changing curvatures and subtle balance resulting from the complex diminishing profile. The traditional sword schools use differently shaped wooden swords in accordance with their particular strategies and techniques.

By the last day of August, a Saturday, all of the bokken for the movie had already been shipped and I was catching up a little on regular scheduled orders. Even though I had labored most weekends, I worked and worked into the late summer afternoon of a dying August. Little adjustments needed to be made in the sharpening fixtures and the sharpening area needed to be rearranged to accommodate the new procedures.

Only as the sun set and the day ended did it occur to me that a major transformation had occurred. It didn't surprise me that this all happened in the month of August, but it did please me immensely. About mid-month, in with all the other work, I had made a wooden sword as a reference piece. It was a spectacular hard and dense piece of hickory with both red and white colors. My finishing cuts were not particularly refined, but the weapon's shape was beautiful and the finished effect was a sword of very good presence and style. Upon close examination, no scratch pattern was evident but instead, hundreds and hundreds of clean tiny facets made up its surface rather than a dulled sanded surface. Its date was August 14, 2002. As it turns out, I had counted the number of cuts necessary to fair out that weapon. It was one thousand and twenty seven. One thousand and twenty seven little cuts with three different hand planes, a small spoke shave, a carving knife, and a small draw knife with a fearful edge had finished that bokken. No sandpaper had touched it. It was sealed with teak oil and glistens with a sort of archaic beauty all its own, as if it is both brand new and hundreds of years old.

Note
* This article describes the developments in the Kingfisher shop that came out of an order of wooden swords in the summer of 2002 by Warner Studios for a Hollywood production, "The Last Samurai."

Reference
Yumoto, J. (1958). *The samurai sword: A handbook.* Tokyo: Charles E. Tuttle.

index

Agency for Cultural Affairs, 7
Ainu migration, 82
Ainu sword (emushi), 84, 86–87, 90
Arai Hakuseki, 84–86
armor-piercing dagger (yoroidoushi), 31, 33
Azuchi-Momoyama Era, 29, 33
back of a sword (mune), 4, 35, 45–46, 59, 99
belt cord fitting (kurigata), 41, 48, 55–57, 59
base of blade (yakidashi), 18
blade carving (horimono), 13, 17, 24
bow and arrow (yumi), 3, 81, 83
bushi warrior caste, 6
cavalry saber, 2, 5
categories of bladed weaponry, 7, 21, 28, 33
criminal corpse, 60–61, 77
dating swords, 2, 29, 85, 95
decorative engraving, 17, 19
deity of swordsmith, 3, 25
dressing for swords (koshiraewere), 28
dried ink (sekkaboku), 17
Edo Era, 29, 33, 36
fake signature (agimei), 33
folding, 21–23, 33
forging process, 3–4, 21–22, 33, 37, 95
gasket (seppa), 32
government issue sword, 37
grain (hada), 4, 6
grooves (hi), 16–17, 19
halberd (naginata), 3, 16, 21, 28, 33, 35–36
handle of sword (tsuka), 3, 5, 27–30, 32–33, 35, 38, 59

Haniwa clay figure, 83
hardened edge (ashi), 18
Heian Era, 2, 35, 85, 90
Hokkaido, 82, 84–85
iaido, 4–5, 11, 40
iaijutsu, 4
kendo, 4, 8
kenjutsu, 4, 8, 40, 77
kitae forging, 22
knife-sized sword (tanto), 2, 4, 21, 28–34, 86
Kofun Era, 83
legalities of swords, 1–2, 7, 9–11
lighting effect on swordmaking, 95, 99
longsword (katana), 2–3, 8, 20–21, 24, 28–29, 33, 37, 61, 86, 89, 90–91
Masamune, 12
Meiji Restoration, 61, 78, 95
metal ends (ishizuki), 35–36
metal sleeve (habaki), 24, 32, 42, 45, 47–49, 52–53, 59
metal tips (fuchigane), 27
military sword (gunto), 6, 36–38
Mino School, 23–24
Nanbokucho Era, 29, 35–36
Nara Era, 29
new sword (shinshakuto), 9, 12
Nihon Bijutsu Token Hozon Kyokai (NBTHK), 5–12
Nihonto Museum, 9
point of sword (kissaki), 15, 18, 28, 59, 99
polishing, 3–4, 9, 18, 24, 47, 98, 100
quality classification of swords, 9, 12, 22, 28, 61
registration, 2, 8, 10–12

registration papers (origami), 9–12
samurai sword (nihonto), 1–3, 5–12
sash (atsu), 80, 84–86, 89–91
Satsuma Rebellion, 95
scabbard (saya), 3, 24, 32, 36, 40–59, 89–91
shaman, 85, 91
shape of sword (sugata), 17–18
shaving wood process, 44, 96, 98, 100
short sword (wakizashi), 2, 16, 30, 33, 43, 59, 61, 84, 86, 89–90
Siberia, 81–82
smelting, 9, 12
Soshu School, 23–24
spear (yari), 20–21, 28, 33–35, 91
Sword and the Same, 84, 86
sword characteristics (hataraki), 15, 18
sword guard (tsuba), 3, 24, 27, 32, 89–91
tang (nakago), 15, 17–18, 23–24, 34–35, 59, 89
tempering, 16, 21–24, 29, 33, 37
tempering line (hamon), 4, 6, 15–18, 22–24
tempering pattern, 18, 24
test cutter (suemonoshi), 61
test cutting (tameshigiri), 60–79
tip of sword (boshi), 18
tracing of blade (oshigata), 15–19
traditional iron (tamahagane), 4–5, 9, 12, 22
US occupation, 4, 8, 11
value of sword, 1, 6, 8–10, 12–13, 97
Visible Human, 62
wood sanding process, 47, 56–57, 96–97
woodworking by Ainu, 81, 86
World War II, 4, 6, 8, 37–38
Yamashiro School, 23
Yamato School, 23–24
Yayoi Period, 81–83
Zaimokuza battlefield, 77
zink-aluminum alloy sword (mogito), 11

Printed in Great Britain
by Amazon